TEACHING
E·T·H·I·C·S

❖

An Interdisciplinary Approach

TEACHING
E·T·H·I·C·S

❖

An Interdisciplinary Approach

Edited by

Robert B. Ashmore
& William C. Starr

Marquette University Press
Milwaukee, Wisconsin

CONTENTS

Appendices

PREFACE

This book is the second volume published by the Center for Ethics Studies as an outcome of grant activity supported by the National Endowment for the Humanities. The first collection of essays, also co-edited by Professor William Starr and myself, appeared in 1991--the final product of an NEH award that enabled us to conduct a two-year program in ethics education at Marquette University. That book, titled *Ethics Across the Curriculum: The Marquette Experience*, contains fourteen essays written by Marquette University faculty from a variety of disciplines who participated in the program. It is available by writing to the Center.

In September, 1991 Professor Starr and I received a second two-year grant for $194,000 to support a "Midwest Program in Ethics Education." This time faculty from a five-state area of the upper midwest were selected to participate in institutes conducted over two summers in 1992 and 1993. We sought the widest possible mix of participants and, as a result, grants were offered to men and women from both two-year and four-year institutions, public and private, who represented some fifteen disciplines across the academic spectrum. (See the appendix for a list of the summer institute participants.) Consequently, twenty professors from Minnesota, Iowa, Wisconsin, Illinois and Michigan came together at Marquette University for an intensive six-week introduction to ethical theory in June and July of 1992.

Sharing the teaching responsibilities with Starr and myself were visiting scholars Richard Kraut (University of Illinois at Chicago), Ralph McInerny (Notre Dame), Thomas Hill (North Carolina), and David Lyons (Cornell). Each of these four lectured on one of the great philosophical works by Aristotle, Aquinas, Kant, and Mill that were discussed over the course of the institute. That summer's project had begun with a reading of my own *Building a Moral System* and concluded with *After Virtue* by Alasdair MacIntyre.

Coming back to Marquette in the summer of 1993, these same participants were now engaged in application of ethical theories to contemporary problem areas. Taking advantage of the diverse disciplinary specializations of the participants, we project directors assigned each of them an active role in the analysis of cases and critique of essays that ranged over topics such as professional/client relationships, deception, informed consent, privacy and confidentiality, individual and collective responsibility, the occupational/ordinary morality distinction and other issues in applied ethics.

Using as our core text for this second summer program an anthology edited by Joan Callahan titled *Ethical Issues in Professional Life*, we invited Callahan to join us during one week of the institute. In other weeks the visiting lecturers included Norman Bowie (Minnesota), Peter French (Trinity), Patricia Werhane (Loyola of Chicago), and Thomas Donaldson (Georgetown). As the 1993 session drew to a close, we laid plans for a volume of essays written by the participants that would be a companion to the earlier published book.

What is to be found in the chapters that follow is a diverse set of reflections on the ways that moral philosophy can be integrated with the subject matter of disciplines across the curriculum. Our program director at the National Endowment suggested that lead-off essays might explain the rationale for selecting Aristotle, Aquinas, Kant and Mill as foundational sources for the two-year project. As a consequence, I have contributed an essay on the enduring relevance of Aristotle and Aquinas to ethical enquiry. And my co-project director has written on Kant and Mill.

The success of this whole endeavor, needless to say, derives in the first instance from support provided to our efforts by the administration of Marquette University, which encouraged creation of the Center for Ethics Studies in 1988 and has followed up with unstinting cooperation in all our projects during the years since. Worthy of special mention in this regard are William Leahy, S.J., Executive Vice President, Francis Lazarus, Vice President for Academic Affairs, Thaddeus Burch, S.J., Dean of the Graduate School, Lynn Miner, Director of Research Support, and John Treloar, S.J., Chair of the Department of

Philosophy.

Both the first and the second grants from the National Endowment for the Humanities were awarded with the invaluable assistance of Dr. Judith Jeffrey Howard at the Endowment office. No words adequately express our appreciation for her counsel as well as her enthusiasm for the work that we have undertaken with NEH support.

Dr. Suzanne Wilson-Davis, whose skills helped to fashion the successful second grant proposal, and Joy Poskozim, our secretary and office manager, also deserve special thanks. Her three years of service to the Center for Ethics Studies concluding upon graduation from Marquette University, Joy's final project has been the production of this book.

It is our hope that this volume will contribute to the educational objective the entire grant project envisioned, namely, a deepened commitment among educators to integration of moral enquiry with all fields of study in the academy.

Robert B. Ashmore

Essays

ARISTOTLE AND AQUINAS ON THE GOOD LIFE

Robert B. Ashmore
Department of Philosophy
Marquette University

It is a remarkable fact that, after more than two thousand years of accumulated reflection on the moral life, writings of a Greek philosopher in the 4th century B.C. and of a medieval cleric in the 13th century A.D. continue to provide uniquely appropriate starting points for ethical enquiry. Aristotle's *Nicomachean Ethics* is almost universally acknowledged to be the most important treatise ever composed on the subject. And Thomas Aquinas, an Italian priest of the Dominican Order, is recognized not only as the most penetrating interpreter of that Aristotelian tradition, but also as one who achieved an unparalleled synthesis of faith and reason, integrating the doctrines of Christian revelation with the deliverances of our natural understanding and experience.

Their place in the college curriculum today is part of the ongoing debate concerning the wisdom of teaching ethical theory, not merely as an elective among philosophy or religion courses, but across all the disciplines. Even where it is conceded that moral thinking is an integral part of education for tasks assumed in every walk of life, there still remains the question concerning which historical figures or schools of thought best serve as introduction to the fundamental issues with which ethics is concerned.

The thesis defended here is that Aristotle and Aquinas constitute two indispensable sources for moral reflection, both because of their enormous influence on the evolution of Western thought and because, in our own day, they present a coherent intellectual approach to enduring questions about how we ought to live our lives both as individuals and in community. As relevant today as it was in any earlier century is the challenge to formulate a consistent and credible conceptual framework for working out solutions to problems inevitably confronted in the professions, as well as in our ordinary lives.

Academic programs that neglect to supply tools for that intellectual task provide at best only a truncated educational experience and, arguably, fail in an essential mission of our schools.

What, it may well be asked, can be more critical to the development of a "liberal" person--in the etymological sense of one whose capacities have been freed for their maximum employment in daily living--than is disciplined familiarization with the process of moral reasoning? In our own culture it has increasingly become apparent that an appalling vacuum exists in any educational enterprise which ignores the centrality of ethical enquiry. Fear of "indoctrination" as well as widespread lack of preparation among faculty for this kind of instruction combine to produce much of this failure. At the same time, there are many academic programs, the one at Marquette University included, in which the enterprise moves forward. And, it will be argued here, the contributions of Aristotle and Aquinas provide perspectives of major importance to that intellectual project.

While situated in cultural environments different in some fundamental respects, Aristotle and Thomas Aquinas share a philosophical conviction about the first question that ethics must address. The starting point must be the end. That is, what both initiates systematic investigation of moral issues and is controlling throughout the enquiry has to be the question of ultimate purpose in human activity. What, finally, do we seek in life? What is it that prompts us to act? The answers that we develop in response to those questions provide a target to aim at; they give direction to our endeavors.

Taking the end of human striving as what justifies acts, rules and institutions is what characterizes those normative theories that are called teleological. And so it is, Aristotle and Aquinas agree, that our investigation concerning what is right and good in all we do must be situated by reference to a goal. Since there is in their view a nonarbitrary determination of that in which the end of human activity consists, we are provided an objective criterion for judging what in both private and public life is suitable as a means to the attainment of that end.

While the skeptically inclined are predisposed to dismiss any prospect of success from this way of proceeding, Aristotle and Aquinas advance the argument that it is both a possible and necessary starting point. What gives order to our individual lives, as well as what makes possible the cooperative enterprise of community-building, is some concept of what actualizes us as human beings, what satisfies our needs and fulfills our most profound aspirations. Not just any conception of the end will do, they maintain, because our theory must be brought to the test of the facts of life. In other words, we must measure the adequacy of our responses concerning the good life by an empirical yardstick. How well do our formulations fit with past and present experience in living?

Although Aquinas will differ from Aristotle in that his Christian faith provides principles not discoverable by the natural light of reason and by empirical evidence, Aquinas carefully distinguishes his theology from his philosophy, and the latter is largely in agreement with Aristotle. We all seek happiness or self-fulfillment, the harmonious satisfaction of human needs and interests adequately considered. Now, views will differ concerning what that consists of, and it is a signal contribution of Aristotle and Aquinas to maintain that the process is one of discovery, not of invention, at its most fundamental level. By this I mean that the foundation of the moral system rests upon inclinations and appetites that are a given. Because we are creatures of a certain kind, possessed of potentialities some of which distinguish us from the rest of nature and others that we share with species of different kinds, and because our recognition of what is good emerges in actualizing those potentialities, both philosophers find an objective ground for moral judgment in this common human nature.

It makes all the difference in the world how one frames the enquiry, and these two philosophers establish perhaps their most important claim for our attention in affirming a moral point of view that squarely confronts subjectivism and relativism, twin scourges of any effort today to defend ethics as a body of knowledge, the product of a search for truth. Whereas contradiction prevails among those who view moral judgments as the equivalent of parochial emotive utterances, while they simultaneously seek reasoned ways of achieving coexistence on this planet, Aristotle and Aquinas propose for consideration another approach. They suggest that we find the common denominator among human inclinations, satisfaction of which is necessary for our survival and prosperity as social beings.

While this approach yields first principles that are universal and nonarbitrary, because they derive from the most basic facts about us as a species, there goes hand in hand with this a realization that circumstances do affect the application of these principles and that legitimately alternative means may be taken to achieving the same end. In short, the discovery of general human tendencies, whose fulfillment would constitute the best of which we are capable, is compatible with acknowledging the trial and error method of establishing truth about human potentialities, as well as accepting the extraordinary variety of particular ways, within limits, that the good life can be pursued.

Forewarned that one should not expect more certainty than the subject matter allows, and that there are inevitable perils in trying to formulate guidelines that admit no exceptions, we are then invited by Aristotle and Aquinas to embark upon an analysis of those generalized conditions that should obtain if human beings are to realize their potential and achieve their end of happiness. The emphasis is on cultivation of those character traits that perfect the individual at various levels of personal and communal life. This scheme, elaborately worked out in terms of virtues and vices and the doctrine of the mean, is another important reason for considering the philosophy of Aristotle and Aquinas. Their contribution, in contrast to other moral theories, is to focus attention not upon observance of rules, bur rather upon self-actualization. Rule theories of a deontological or utilitarian sort take the central question to be, "What should I do?" Bound up with that approach to the moral life is a preoccupation with issues such as duty or obligation, the characteristics of a code of conduct, the justification of exceptions to rules, the determination of priorities among imperatives, and the sanctions reinforcing observance of rules. The emphasis is upon establishing criteria for right action, conceived in terms of a hierarchical structure of principles and rules that a moral agent is duty-bound to obey.

An alternative to this emphasis on rules takes the form of claiming that the prior question does not so much concern what I should *do*, but rather "What kind of person should I *be*?" From this point of view the initial concern is to identify the good of human beings and establish this as a norm of self-actualization. Of course, when we set about becoming a certain kind of person, we do not discard rules or the concept of duty. But the emphasis does shift to a concern with character development, the role played by virtues and vices, and the components in our biological and psychological nature that are affected by and that influence moral growth.

Accordingly, Aristotle and Aquinas would have us consider first the question of virtue, then the role of rules. Rules are derived from and justified in terms of a conception of the good. From this perspective the construction of an overall plan of life presupposes some clear ideas about what an ideal human being is like. Virtue is a key concept in this approach, because the habits or dispositions that are formed in the course of moral development constitute the character of the individual. They determine the pattern of behavior and responses to life situations. The basic insight here is that as a person *is*, so that person *acts*. Since the process of becoming is unending, a practical question faces us at every turn in life: what kind of person *shall* I be?

More than half of Aristotle's *Nicomachean Ethics* concerns formation of habits, the distinction between virtues and vices, and what kinds of excellence can be developed in our knowing and in our desiring. In his commentary on Aristotle's ethics, as well in his own major work, the *Summa Theologiae*, Thomas Aquinas likewise emphasizes the analysis of good and bad dispositions, importantly defending the view that choices here are not arbitrary, because we work from a concept of human nature and of a related ideal to which these habits are instrumental. Since the concern is with action, becoming a good person and behaving as such, the knowledge sought here is practical, not simply theoretical. And since right action requires excellence in our willing and in those passions that move us to act, we need moral as well as intellectual virtues.

Too often those who argue about moral matters get tangled what should remain distinct in our thinking, namely, judging the act and judging the agent who performs the act. Aristotle and Aquinas are clear that a right act may be performed by an agent who is not virtuous but who may do it, say, from a bad motive or even inadvertently. It is also possible for a good person to perform a wrong act, as when someone is inculpably ignorant of some relevant fact in the situation. While the criterion of right action will be the end and what is conducive to that end, one is a virtuous agent only if that person knowingly, willingly and consistently performs right acts and does so because they are right.

These four characteristics of the praiseworthy agent underscore the relevance of Aristotle and Aquinas' discussion of habits and of the intellectual and moral virtues. They also point to the fundamental importance of issues such as responsibility for action and factors like ignorance and compulsion which can mitigate or even destroy the voluntariness of an action. There is much concern today about a trend toward denial of personal responsibility for behavior. What Erich Fromm once labelled the "escape from freedom" is encouraged by those defense attorneys, sociologists and psychologists who virtually embrace strict determinism. Accountability for conduct shifts from choices made by individual agents to environments which necessitate the behavior. What is not apparent to such determinists is the illogic of transferring responsibility to a controlling environment, which we are then encouraged (through our choices?) to control and ameliorate.

The contemporary debate about freedom and necessity in human action thus provides yet another warrant for considering the moral perspective of Aristotle and Aquinas. For, both of them present nuanced analyses of factors that contribute to voluntariness and involuntariness, targeting for particular criticism the easy tendency to write off habituated behavior as unfree. Aristotle commonsensically notes that, of course, it is difficult to act contrary to one's dispositions. But, that just reinforces the importance of cultivating the right sorts of habits and of making wise decisions about the environmental influences that help to shape attitudes and preferences. Indeed, the discussion of ethics seamlessly leads us into politics, since we achieve our self-actualization as social beings whose life in community can flourish only under sound laws.

With his distinction between that which is "just by nature" and what is "just by convention" Aristotle in Book V of the *Nicomachean Ethics* adumbrates the much more fully developed philosophy of law found in Thomas Aquinas. It is Aquinas' Treatise on Law, found in *Summa Theologiae*, I-II, Questions 90-97, that contains the classic statement of natural law theory. A central issue in the history of legal philosophy concerns the conflict between two opposing views on the nature of law. Positivism holds that law is whatever has been determined or "posited" by the sovereign legislative power in the community. There is no necessary connection between law and morality, since the command of the sovereign establishes what law is, which may not at all correspond with what law ought to be. By contrast, natural law theory maintains that law must be viewed as an instrument for achieving the human good. Accordingly, the basic principles of law are discovered rather than made by humans. Objective facts about what humans need in order to realize their potential for the good life are accessible to human reason. These requirements of our nature provide a standard for measuring the adequacy of institutions and of statutes enacted in various social arrangements.

Aquinas not only provides the historically most significant statement of natural law theory, but he situates it within a larger framework that contrasts with Aristotle. This is because, as a Christian, Aquinas believes that God has revealed truths to human beings, and God's creatures are destined for a life hereafter that exceeds our natural grasp. Since humans have a "super-natural" as well as a natural goal, and it is by faith that we assent to what God has revealed, the treatment of law in Aquinas' theory extends beyond what philosophers such as Aristotle could have considered. In addition to natural law and human temporal law, Aquinas discusses divine law, revealed imperfectly in the Old Testament and then perfectly with the coming of Jesus Christ.

Inasmuch as Aquinas is always careful to distinguish between that which "unaided" human reason can naturally discover about the moral order, in contrast to what is known because of God revealing, one encounters little difficulty in undertaking separate consideration of his philosophical and of his theological views. Consequently, students of Aquinas have the twofold advantage of a conceptually sophisticated natural law theory as well as a clear statement of how that philosophical position can be integrated within a larger faith-enhanced totality. Aquinas' synthesis of reason and revelation is a monumental intellectual achievement of the Middle Ages. But, even for those who are not Christian and who may even be atheist, there is to be found in Aquinas the articulation of a naturalistic foundation for legal principles that has proved fundamental in our own day to the defense of human rights and to justifications of disobedience against oppressive legal structures.

Absent some conceptual framework such as that provided by Aquinas, one would be at a loss to account for charges of "crimes against humanity" directed at Nazis in the Nuremberg trials. Or the resistance campaign of Martin Luther King that was grounded upon recognition of a "higher law." Or the attempts by organizations like Amnesty International to protect people in various parts of the world from abuse of their fundamental rights. Implied in all such efforts is the view, centuries ago worked out by Aquinas, that human law must serve an end that is not the mere product of power. Unjust laws, commands that are in conflict with the common good, are not binding. Assessments of and support for enactments of human legislators are necessarily linked to concepts of what law ought to be, discoverable in reflection upon what is needed to survive and prosper in human community.

Justice, the virtue that is concerned with conformity of action to law as it ought to be, occupies an understandably central place in the Aristotelian and Thomistic scheme of virtues. Other moral virtues address challenges that human beings face in coping with fears and dangers (courage) or in satisfying appetites for food and sex and the like (temperance). Fine-grained distinction of specific drives and inclinations produces in Aristotle and Aquinas a fascinating moral psychology of good and bad habits. Their "doctrine of the mean" provides a method for identification of the wide range of dispositions that are or are not perfective of human inclinations. Honesty, patience, gratitude, modesty and a host of other qualities constitute moderating expressions of impulses and passions that are in themselves morally neutral. It is only in the context of time and place and other circumstances that assessment can be made concerning what is appropriate behavior.

It is for this reason, Aristotle and Aquinas argue, that intellectual and moral virtues constitute what we might call a "package deal." One function of reason in the practical order is to discern the relative mean in the moral virtues. That is, the person of prudence or practical wisdom is one who knows the various circumstances of the particular situation and correctly judges what is called for. Excess and deficiency name responses that are at opposing extremes from the mean. So, for example, in the matter of giving money one may be stingy or profligate, identified as vices opposed to the virtue of generosity. However, what is reasonable and hence virtuous in sharing of resources will depend on context, e.g., one's own financial capabilities, the needs of possible recipients, and so forth.

A key insight here is that no general principle is capable of self-application. Experience in living as well as the good example of others facilitate those prudential judgments that are required here and now and that can only be approximated in more abstract norms. Exceptions to rules are an unavoidable feature of life, in recognition of the fact that any general proposition can only take account of what happens for the most part. The infinite variety of circumstances in which persons might find themselves demands that individualized judgment must fill the gap.

Illustrative of the contemporary relevance and suggestive power of this classical virtue theory is the discussion in Aquinas and Aristotle of a virtue called amiability or friendliness. (Cf. Aquinas, *Summa Theologiae*, II-II, Questions 114-116 and Aristotle, *Nicomachean Ethics*, Book IV, Ch. 6.) I select this virtue because it is fast disappearing from our public life, and we are all immensely the poorer because of that. How often today we note the growing loss of civility, that refinement of manners which manifests respect for one another. In politics, in sports, in news gathering, in popular entertainment--in virtually every area of social interaction--there is increasing tolerance of and consequent exhibition of incivility. Where formerly it was insisted that courtesy moderate the ambitious pursuit of one's objectives, there is now a no-holds-barred philosophy regarding self-expression and the desire to succeed. Perversely there is even a suggestion that young people must mature to the realization that "nice guys finish last" and that restraint in self-expression is unwholesome inhibition.

Contrast the crudeness in our public arenas today with what Aristotle and Aquinas say about the virtue of friendliness. It behooves us, they argue, to act in a becoming manner toward one another. After all, it is difficult to live together in community unless we try to be agreeable. We must be sensitive to the joy or sorrow that we cause others by our behavior. They go further and state that a certain debt toward fellow humans requires us in justice to treat them amicably. That debt which links friendliness to justice consists in owing others that which they deserve, giving them what is their due. The core message is that their due is respect. The virtuous person, Aristotle tells us, "will act by the standard of what is noble and beneficial. For his concern will be with the pleasures and pains that are found in social relations." Alien to this character trait is a kind of selfish indifference to others that today masquerades as self-reliance. Survival requires, according to the worldly wise, that we cultivate a ruggedness that yields no advantage to the adversary. And herein lies the essential fallacy. Our nature is social; we need one another. Hence, it cannot be normative that we construe the relationship as self versus others.

Recall that the point of moral enquiry is to achieve an ideal, to discover the best in us and to actualize *that* potential. Turning this philosophy on its head, the brutish message today is that we succeed by maximizing the *worst* of which we are capable. Of course, both Aristotle and Aquinas realize that one can go to excess in being pleasant. As with all the virtues, so with friendliness there is an extreme opposed to the virtue that goes beyond what is due in cordiality toward others. The obsequious always praise, even when a good word is not warranted. Flattery sins against friendliness by putting up with everything, by tolerating and even casting in a good light what deserves to be condemned. Obsequiousness violates truth and justice in exaggerating the pleasure to which others are entitled.

The opposite vice is quarrelsomeness. Here the person is one who always finds fault. Excessively contradictory and contentious, the moral defect of quarrelsome people is their settled disposition to be disagreeable. This reveals itself in reluctance to acknowledge what is good in others, preferring rather to emphasize the negative. Grouchy people oppose everything and seem grieved by others' good fortune. Quick to spot whatever is imperfect in those among whom they dwell, such ill-humored people will foment discord when they cannot find it pre-existing, and they will encourage competition and mutual suspicion among those who might otherwise make common cause. Although the opposite vice of obsequiousness is objectionable, quarrelsomeness is even more odious, since it is more opposed to the virtue, friendliness, which tends to please rather than to displease.

Today the aggressive, the foul-mouthed, and the negative prevail to the extent that we oddly take more interest in bad news than good; we admire the ruthless critic; we are amused by inane and prurient talk show hosts; we harbor an insatiable appetite for violence in athletic contests; and we stand in awe of those who humiliate and ridicule. Aristotle and Aquinas would view such tendencies as a disease of the soul. And a society such as ours, which increasingly accords celebrity status to demeaning entertainers, meanspirited journalists, and vulgar athletes would surely be diagnosed as pathological.

In ways similar to what has been done here with their tripartite analysis of friendliness and its opposite extremes, we can gain perspective on much else in contemporary life by carefully considering the catalogue of virtues and vices found in the moral philosophy of Aristotle and Aquinas. Passage of time does not diminish the relevance of their reflections on purposes and tendencies that endure in humanity's various experiments in living. In the modern era what began as a necessary and wholesome emancipation of people from authoritarian political and religious institutions has devolved into a cult of individualism. The autonomous rational being, recognized as possessed of rights and entitled to participate in decisions of state is one thing. The narcissistic deification of an isolate self for whom social arrangements are secondary and artificial is quite another. The latter erects egoism into a virtue. One form for its expression is in economic theory, where a capitalist ontology of the individual argues that each of us stands to the other in a necessarily adversarial relationship.

Egocentricity is supplied a veneer of rationality with the argument that, after all, everybody does what they most want to do and, if we don't act selfishly, who else can be expected to look out for us in this dog-eat-dog world. What in earlier times might have been regarded as social virtues, inspiring us to acts of solidarity and commiseration in the misfortune of others, are too often nowadays taken to be forms of weakness that cause us to be shrouded in misplaced feelings of guilt about routine inequities in consumption and distribution.

In our own society such preoccupation with self moves us to elaborate self-deceptions about the acquisition of wealth and power. Privilege is seen to be earned and deserved, when in fact much of it is inherited or is otherwise a matter of luck. Nevertheless, many people, born on third base, act as if they hit a triple.

The "virtue of selfishness" in international relations empowers us to justify consumption of a disproportionate share of the world's natural resources, exploit foreign peoples as cheap labor forces, and view underdeveloped countries as convenient markets for dangerous products like cigarettes and military weaponry. In the classroom a marketing ideology explains that advertising does not create wants; it simply informs people about products that will satisfy their already preexisting wants. And a not so subtle form of racism assumes that, in the grip of our economic colonialism, populations beyond our borders are really better off than they otherwise would be. In any case, it is "our" oil, to give just one example, and it will turn into our killing field if any foreign power threatens our access.

Within the framework of an Aristotelian and Thomistic moral theory what is most disturbing about this solipsism, domestic or international, is its denial of the essential relatedness of our being. Community, which Aristotle and Aquinas consider a *sine qua non* of human perfectibility, loses its ground when the interests of self and of others are viewed disjunctively--me versus you. Aristotle and Aquinas argue that our true advantage is not obtained at the expense of or in disregard of others. And it is the goal of politics to serve the moral ideal through legislation of some morality, though not all.

Contrary to a mindlessly repeated assertion, we can legislate morality, and we do. We require or forbid by law much that we judge to be morally right or wrong. We prohibit murder and rape and theft. We require child support, water purification and elementary education. Laws also prescribe penalties for those who seek unfair gain in violation of the social contract. Strange as it may sound to the modern ear, there is much to consider in this classical claim: the aim of politics is to produce virtuous citizens.

Today we learn that social programs such as Head Start are already too late. Studies reveal that even at two years of age children have been exposed to irreparable harm. This is not excessively difficult to grasp when one considers the social disintegration reported daily in the news: cocaine addicted babies delivered to teenage mothers; half the children in major urban areas born out of wedlock; youthful gangs responsible for an increasing percentage of "adult" felonies. Aristotle and Aquinas would suggest to students of ethics and politics that the proper beginning makes a great difference, perhaps the whole difference. The importance of being well brought up is underscored in their notion of the necessary collaboration between family, educational institutions, and the state in instilling good habits in the very young. If we have been well brought up, we will find pleasure in appropriate things. But, if our character has been badly formed, we will take pleasure in that which is not by nature pleasant. The malleability of human passions means that anything can be a source either of pleasure or pain, depending on what kind of person we have become.

Timidity in defending clear moral aims in the structure of the family, in education, and in political agenda is part of the inevitable fallout from relativism and the abandonment of reason in value formation. How can one defend what is capable only of being baldly asserted? Untutored feelings wed to the notion that all value judgments are equally valid is a recipe for disaster that Aristotle and

Aquinas well understood. Appetite for a noble life is absent in those who have no experience of it, and the experience is impossible if physical and psychological and social conditions have deformed the individual's capacities. Since such crippling predispositions can stunt one's potential for the good life as early as the womb, Aristotle and Aquinas would have us take seriously their contention that moral education must be a common concern, that "to obtain the right training for virtue from youth up is difficult, unless one has been brought up under the right laws." (*Nicomachean Ethics*, Bk. X, Ch. 9) Subjectivism and value relativism, naturally, make hopeless such a project. Nothing can count as a better or worse reason for our choices; they are all on a democratic par. Ironically, the abandonment of rationality in defense of moral judgments leaves contemporary society with nothing but imposition of will as the deciding factor. Yet such arbitrary imposition was precisely what egalitarianism was supposed to prevent.

The thrust of this essay has been to suggest that, both in introducing the philosophical initiate to ethical theory and in applying critical tools of moral reasoning to analysis of contemporary social problems, the conceptual frameworks developed by Aristotle and Aquinas are of very great value. At the same time, they themselves exhibited toward other thinkers the attitude that they would have us display toward their own work, that is, an openness to consideration that does not preclude the careful weighing of alternatives. Both Aristotle and Aquinas approached the subject matter always disposed to acknowledge and assimilate the best insights of their predecessors and contemporaries. One cannot read the writings of either of them without becoming familiar with every other significant view held in their times.

It is in this same spirit that we today should study Aristotle and Aquinas. Their work is a resource of fundamental importance, but it should be weighed in the encounter with other diverse and sometimes conflicting theories. As Aristotle himself said concerning the frame of mind with which one should approach ethical enquiry, "Every person has something of his own to contribute to the finding of the truth."

KANT, MILL, AND THE SUPREME PRINCIPLE OF MORALITY

William C. Starr
Department of Philosophy
Marquette University

Both Aristotle and Aquinas thought that it was essential to live a good life. Aristotle believed that the way to live a life of human excellence was to act in accordance with the eleven virtues he listed in his *Nicomachean Ethics*. Aquinas thought that one would achieve the best life by obeying the natural law and loving God unconditionally. Robert Ashmore in the previous essay in this volume has developed the views of Aristotle and Aquinas.

Kant and Mill both believe that one should live a good life. Yet their approach to ethics is different than both Aristotle and Aquinas in a fundamental way. Kant and Mill wish to develop their ethical theories respectively by promulgating and then defending a supreme principle of morality. Although they both believe that one should act virtuously as Aristotle held, their focus is on the notion of fidelity to principle. If one acts consistently in accordance with the supreme principle of morality, then one will be an ethical person. Yet Kant and Mill developed and argued for quite different supreme principles of morality. First, let us turn our attention to the ethics of Immanuel Kant and next to the ethics of John Stuart Mill.

Kant and the Categorical Imperative

Immanuel Kant was a German philosopher who lived from 1724-1804. He is the most famous representative of a tradition in moral philosophy known as deontological ethics. Deontological ethics holds that moral reasoning should be based on whether a moral principle can be justified on its own merits. This means that the ethical principle must pass moral muster independent of whether good consequences will likely follow from adhering to it. Good consequences, of course, are desirable whether one is discussing personal well being, the public interest of society, or general happiness of the world. To deny the value of good consequences resulting from ethical decision making would be incredulous.

However, for Kant and the deontological tradition in ethics, desirable consequences are *not* the standard of moral appraisal in this ethical tradition. Kant holds that notions other than consequences determine the moral worth of an ethical decision. What are they? It is this issue which will now be discussed.

Kant makes a fundamental and unprovable claim about human nature. For Kant's ethical theory to be considered credible, this claim must be accepted by the reader. Kant holds that human nature is basically good in the following way. *Human beings, if they lacked particular wants and needs tailored to their own individual situation, would always act morally.* If one does accept this view about persons, then Kant believes his moral philosophy is an inevitable outcome of this position. It is time to discover how this is the case.

Kant writes, "It is impossible to conceive anything at all in the world, or even out of it, which can be taken as good without qualification, except a *good will"* (Immanuel Kant, *Groundwork of the Metaphysic of Morals,* trans. H.J. Paton, Harper & Row, New York, 1964, p. 61; hereafter *Groundwork*). One who possesses a good will always acts in accordance with the moral law. One simply has no desire to act unethically. Kant believes that if everyone acted in accordance with a good will, the world would be a perfectly moral universe. Elsewhere he calls such a moral universe a "kingdom of ends" (*Groundwork*, pp. 100-101). He passionately notes that simply knowing the moral virtues and acting upon them is not enough to be a fully moral person. Kant writes,

> Moderation in affections and passions, self-control, and sober reflection are not only good in many respects: they may even seem to constitute part of the *inner* worth of a person. Yet they are far from being properly described as good without qualification (however unconditionally they have been commended by the ancients). For without the principles of a good will they may become exceedingly bad; and the very

coolness of a scoundrel makes him, not merely more dangerous, but also immediately more abominable in our eyes than we should have taken him to be without it. (*Groundwork,* pp. 61-62)

The reader may be wary. What is the essence of a good will? Specifically, how should one act if one wishes to make decisions in accordance with a good will? Is the good will something more than a hopelessly abstract concept which has little if any relationship with actual human beings who have to make concrete decisions in the real world? These questions must be answered if one is to make sense of Kant's ethical theory. In order to do this, Kant's analysis of duty and the categorical imperative (Kant's supreme principle of morality) must now be carefully discussed.

For Kant, a person with a good will acts in accordance with duty. One's duty is the core of one's moral obligation. If one has a duty to do X, then one must do X. One is morally obligated to do X in the strongest possible terms. So, for example, if one has a duty to tell the truth, one has incurred a strong moral obligation to tell the truth. This will become clearer as Kant's moral philosophy further unfolds. As will be discovered shortly, one's fundamental moral duty is to act consistently with the categorical imperative. However, before a discussion of the categorical imperative takes place, it is helpful to further discuss the concept of "duty" in Kant.

The best way to understand "duty" in Kant is to contrast it with another Kantian term "inclination." For Kant, the term "inclination" is very broad. It encompasses virtually all of our wants, needs, and desires. So, if I want to go to the movies tonight, I will plan my time accordingly so I will be able to do so at the time I wish. If I wish to be a philosophy professor, I will plan my course of study for the required number of years so I will be able to accomplish my long range goal. These two examples indicate that inclinations may be short term or long term. Inclinations which one has are not universal. They are particular to me. No two people have exactly the same set of inclinations, but we all have them. Inclinations may be nonmoral (going to the movies), moral (live an honest life), or immoral (live the life of a thief).

For Kant the supreme principle of morality cannot be based on inclinations for two decisive reasons. First, there is no guarantee that our inclinations will be moral in nature. As mentioned above, while some of our inclinations are moral, some are nonmoral and some may well be immoral. Inclinations are psychological in nature. That is, they reflect whatever we desire at a particular point in time. If an inclination happened to be a moral one (e.g. tell the truth), it would be an ethically happy accident. There is nothing in the development of our inclinations which require that they be ethical. Kant is opposed to developing a theory of moral philosophy on the basis of contingent psychological propensities.

Second, Kant believes that the supreme principle of morality must be *universal*. This tenet of Kant's ethics is fundamental. The supreme principle of morality must be applicable to all people at all times under all circumstances. Such a universal state of affairs cannot be accomplished by inclinations. That is impossible since inclinations are particularized to a specific individual at a given time.

At this point Kant makes the move upon which his moral philosophy turns. It is this. If a person lacked inclinations, what would be left? His response to this question is that a *good will* would remain in place because without inclinations to lead them astray, all humans are naturally good people and wish to act in accordance with a morally good life. For Kant living a morally good life consistent with a good will is to do one's moral duty and not act on the basis of one's inclinations. This is the role of "duty" in Kant's ethical theory. Of course, something is still missing here. What is one's moral duty? That question needs to be addressed.

Kant holds that the supreme principle of morality is what he calls the *categorical imperative*. It is an imperative in the sense that it commands one to act morally. It is categorical in the sense that it is unconditional. That is, it is not dependant upon other conditions holding. If the imperative was conditioned on other circumstances, it would be called a hypothetical imperative. The difference between the two types of imperatives can be illustrated in the following way:

Hypothetical Imperative: If Y holds, do X.

Categorical Imperative: Do X.

Morality for Kant cannot be based on hypothetical imperatives since a universal ethics cannot occur if the imperative ("do X") is based on prior conditions. A prior condition (e.g. If it is to my advantage, tell the truth) may or may not hold. What is clear is that the condition "if it is to my advantage" will not always occur in all situations at all times for all people. Thus, a universal ethics cannot be constructed on the basis of hypothetical imperatives.

The case is different for the categorical imperative. The claim "do X" is unconditioned. From a moral perspective, one must do X whenever one is called to do X. The categorical imperative is indeed universal. Since there are no prior conditions which may or may not obtain, a principle can be constructed which can apply to all individuals at all times under all situations. For Kant, therefore, a supreme principle of morality which accurately describes a person acting in accordance with a good will by doing one's duty must be a categorical imperative. Is there such a categorical imperative which can serve as the supreme principle of morality? If so, what is it?

Kant holds that such a categorical imperative does exist. He formulates it in five different ways. The two most well known formulations will be quoted and will be discussed in order to discern how the categorical imperative actually works. For Kant the two most important components of the categorical imperative are 1) that it is universal in application, and 2) it requires a certain mode of conduct in all of our actions which have moral import. This mode of conduct he calls "respect for persons." Let us have a look at these two formulations of the categorical imperative.

I "Universal" formulation:

"Act only on that maxim through which you can at the same time will that it should become a universal law." (*Groundwork*, p. 88)

II "Respect for persons" formulation:

"Act in such a way that you always treat humanity, whether in your own person or in the person of any other, never simply as a means, but always at the same time as an end." (*Groundwork*, p. 96)

The best way to explain the categorical imperative is to look at an example of its application. Consider the issue of truth telling. Kant holds that telling the truth can be universalized (formulation I) and telling the truth shows respect for persons (formulation II). If everyone told the truth as a universal proposition, the world would function quite nicely. We would live in a world without fraud, without deception, without misrepresentation, and without uncertainty. This would be most desirable. People could plan their lives and activities without having to be concerned with whether information which they relied upon was truthful. Society can function harmoniously if we all tell the truth to each other. Thus, truth telling can be universalized.

Telling the truth also shows respect for persons. Telling the truth to another promotes trust and integrity. It allows the person being told the truth to proceed knowing that the information forthcoming is accurate. Can one have a genuine relationship with another if one is constantly wondering if one was told the truth? Can one trust another if one is constantly wondering if the truth was told? Can one be said to be treated with respect if one is told the truth only if it is in the another's interest to do so? The answer to all of these questions is "NO!" For Kant, the categorical imperative, especially the "respect for persons" version, is the moral bottom line. That is, it is *always* morally wrong to act in a way that does not show respect for persons. Hence, Kant believes he has shown that the categorical imperative is the first principle of morality, and that it is universal, exceptionless, noncontextual, and atemporal.

The importance of Kant for moral reasoning and for living a good life is as follows. Kant gives the sensitive morally reflective citizen who wants to act ethically a clear test for ascertaining whether he or she is doing so. It is more a negative test than a positive test. The reason this is the case is that if one acts in accordance with the categorical imperative, one is likely though not necessarily doing the best ethical action. However, if one does not act in accordance with the categorical imperative, then for Kant it is certain that that individual is not acting in a morally acceptable manner. It is fair to say that the categorical imperative itself is not exhaustive of morality itself. One would need an entire complex set of moral principles, rules, precepts, and correct applications of these principles, rules, and precepts in particular cases for individuals, organizations, and nations to have a truly complete theory of ethics. Whether such an exhaustive theory could ever be developed is an open question. What is powerful, philosophically attractive, and reasonable about the categorical imperative is that it gives one a bona fide test of whether one is or is not acting ethically in a way that shows equal respect and concern for every member of the human community. For that we are all indebted to the ethics of Immanuel Kant.

John Stuart Mill and the Principle of Utility

John Stuart Mill is a 19th century British philosopher who lived from 1806-1863. Mill, like Kant, espouses a supreme principle of morality. Mill agrees with Aristotle that one should be virtuous in the way a person lives his or her life. Mill agrees with Aquinas that an important principle of morality is to support the common good. In fact we shall discover that Mill elevates this principle in a slightly different form to the status of a supreme principle of morality. Mill believes in agreement with Kant that a supreme principle of morality is needed as a test of whether one is acting morally. Also, Mill places great emphasis on the idea of the supreme principle of morality as a final arbitrator when two secondary moral principles come into conflict as they on occasion surely do. More on this later.

Mill is asking the following question. As a member of society what is my primary moral obligation? Mill in answering this question places a paramount emphasis on the importance of helping create the best possible community. So, for Mill, the primary moral obligation of an ethically reflective person is do precisely those actions which will best maximize the collective interest of the community. Of course, other moral principles such as Kant's fundamental moral tenet of "respect for persons" are extremely important for Mill because if we respect each other, the community will benefit. However, in the final analysis enhancing the quality of life in the community takes precedence for Mill over competing ethical principles. This is a key difference between Mill and Kant. The concept of respect for persons is an extremely individualistic form of ethics. As we shall discover, the ethics of utility, as Mill formulates it, is more society based.

Mill characterizes the principle of utility, his supreme principle of morality, as follows:

> The creed which accepts as the foundation of morals "utility" or the "greatest happiness principle" holds that actions are right in proportion as they tend to promote happiness; wrong as they tend to produce the reverse of happiness. By happiness is intended pleasure and the absence of pain; by unhappiness, pain and the privation of pleasure (Mill, *Utilitarianism*, Hackett Publishing Co., (ed.) George Sher, 1979, p. 7--hereafter *Utilitarianism*).

Two points are worth emphasizing at this time. First, Mill is not advocating an egoistic moral philosophy. That is, he is not suggesting that one ought simply to attempt to maximize one's own happiness whenever one makes an ethical decision. He is advocating the view that the happiness of society is what is paramount. So, an individual should make decisions which maximize societal happiness, not simply one's own individual happiness. Most of the time one's own personal happiness will be in accord with the happiness of the community. That is fine with Mill. After all, everyone counts as a member of the community including the particular decision maker. However, in those cases where there is a conflict between one's personal happiness and the collective happiness of the community, the community comes first.

Thus, Mill is not offering an egoistic theory.

Second, Mill is extremely sensitive to the potential criticism of his theory that if X is pleasurable, then it is acceptable to do X regardless of what that pleasure happens to be. It would be a misreading of Mill to maintain that he espouses such a view. In the literature this has become known as the "swine ethic" objection against Mill's utilitarianism. Here is how he refutes this objection. He notes that when one analyzes pleasure for human beings, one does not simply quantify any pleasure and say that the greatest quantity of pleasure is what we should seek. Mill also maintains that it is essential to analyze the *quality* of a given pleasure as part of moral evaluation.

Mill makes a key distinction between higher and lower pleasures. Consider two examples. First, think of different kinds of music. In particular, note (a) the music of Beethoven, and (b) the music of the current popular rock group Ace of Bass. Mill would maintain that the music of Beethoven represents a higher pleasure, the music of Ace of Bass a lower pleasure. That is, to properly appreciate the complex textured music of Beethoven takes an enormous amount of time and music education. To properly appreciate the simplistic music of Ace of Bass (I've heard it) takes neither. Mill would hold that the music of Beethoven is qualitatively superior to that of Ace of Bass. A society of Beethoven lovers would be a qualitatively better society than a society of Ace of Bass lovers. There is greater utility in the music of Beethoven than in the music of Ace of Bass. Our level of culture and civilization is at a higher level when we understand and appreciate Beethoven. To put this in terms of Mill's utilitarian moral philosophy, the general welfare, public interest, greatest happiness for society, etc. are all enhanced by increased knowledge of the higher pleasure than by the lower pleasure. Not all pleasures for Mill are to weighted equally.

A second example to illustrate the higher/lower pleasure distinction is that of sexual relations. To take two extremes, one can have a sexual relation which is purely casual in nature. There is some pleasure in the act, or it would not be performed. But what sort of pleasure is it? It is short term, transitory, lacks lasting value, lacks continuity with the rest of one's life, and lacks any significance in one's life other than a short term pleasure. It adds virtually nothing to the quality of one's life. Contrast this with sexual relations between two persons genuinely in love. Sexual relations here represent a part of the ongoing process of the enhancement of one's existence. Sexual relations in this case are over the long term, permanent, are of lasting value, and are an integral part of one's life. Sexual relations between two persons in love are an important part of the *quality* of the life of those persons. Needless to say, the first type of sexual relation represents a lower pleasure, the second represents a higher pleasure. As in the music example, the sexual relations example shows that there is far greater utility in a loving long term relationship than a casual transitory relationship.

A person who has experienced both higher and lower pleasures is precisely the person qualified to ascertain which is superior. Mill holds that invariably such a person will prefer the higher pleasure whether the issue is music or sexual relations or anything else. Mill, therefore, opts for a culture and civilization which attempts to maximize higher pleasures for all. When this occurs, utility will be maximized and the community will benefit from such a society of higher pleasure seekers. One can see why Mill was such an advocate of the notion of education for all children, restrictions on working hours, and a supporter of easier access to literature and the arts for all citizens. When these things occur, people have both the education and time to pursue the finer things in life, the higher pleasures. We are all better for this. Mill is at his best here, powerfully arguing for a community to achieve the highest possible level of civilization.

Mill believes that the great majority of time persons know how to act morally. If they do not, this is not from ignorance. It is from weakness of will. However, there will be at times conflicts between two perfectly acceptable moral rules in isolation. It is here when one needs a supreme principle of morality. Otherwise, when moral conflicts occur, we will be in a moral abyss. What to do? Draw straws? Flip a coin? Wait for some sort of natural light of reason? Of course not! If this is the best moral philosophy can do, we may as well turn to astrology or psychics for answers.

Mill at this juncture holds that the supreme principle of morality is the final arbiter of moral conflict, a supreme court of morality. That is, when there are moral conflicts, it is the supreme principle of morality to which one should turn for guidance as to what is the best decision to make in a given case. Does the right to freedom of the press give me the right as a reporter to report the intimate details of one's personal life which that individual does not wish to be publicly known? Here is a genuine conflict between the right to freedom of the press and the right to privacy. Mill would hold in this case that whichever decision maximized utility is the correct decision to make. He would call what I have been calling rights in this example "secondary principles." On the role of the principle of utility in these types of conflicts, Mill cannot be clearer.

> There exists no moral system under which there do not arise unequivocal cases of conflicting obligation. These are the real difficulties, the knotty pines both in the theory of ethics and in the conscientious guidance of personal conduct. If utility is the ultimate source of moral obligations, utility may be invoked to decide between them when their demands are incompatible. We must remember that only in these cases of conflict between secondary principles is it requisite that first principles should be appealed to. There is no case of moral obligation in which some secondary principle is not involved; and if only one, there can seldom be any real doubt which one it is, in the mind of any person by whom the principle itself is recognized (*Utilitarianism*, p. 25).

In conclusion, Mill devoted his moral philosophy to the notion of helping create the best society possible. All sectors of society: individuals; business; education; government; ought to be doing those things which will best maximize the collective welfare of society. We do this by acting in accordance with the key tenets of morality accepted through the ages (keep promises, tell the truth, do not harm others, etc.). Utilitarianism is consistent with ordinary moral intuitions. However, in the small range of cases in which there is moral conflict between moral rules (secondary principles), it is the principle of utility which is the final moral court of appeal. In these cases of conflict, we should choose the alternative which will likely maximize utility.

Both Kant and Mill have had their theories of morality stand the test of time. They both believe a supreme principle of morality is needed. Although they have different supreme principles of morality, solid arguments can be made in defense of both of them. This is as it should be. No moral theory can seriously deny the importance of respecting all persons as members of the moral community (Kant). No moral theory can seriously deny the importance of attempting to develop and maintain the best society possible for all of its members (Mill). Perhaps the "perfect" moral theory will be one which can successfully combine both the categorical imperative and the principle of utility into one internally consistent moral theory. Can such a theory successfully be developed and defended? Now *that* is a most interesting open question.*

*Some of the material for this essay has closely followed parts of my "Ethical Theory and the Teaching of Ethics," in *Ethics Across the Curriculum: The Marquette Experience*, Marquette University Press, 1991, pp. 19-35.

References

Immanuel Kant. *Groundwork of the Metaphysic of Morals*. Trans. H. J. Paton. Harper & Row, 1964.

John Stuart Mill. *Utilitarianism*. Ed. George Sher. Hackett Publishing Co., 1979.

BEYOND PC: THE ETHICS OF CLASSROOM CONTROVERSY

James Arnt Aune
Department of Speech-Theater
St. Olaf College

You are the chair of the Department of English at a major midwestern university. A member of your department, a young woman who specializes in medieval literature, is up for tenure this year. Her student evaluations are excellent, and her publication record is outstanding, including a book from a major university press. She has otherwise distinguished herself as a cooperative colleague, with helpful service on departmental and college committees. Shortly before your department is to send a recommendation to the university tenure committee, the candidate is arrested during an on-campus demonstration against a visiting lecturer. The candidate is a member of a local radical group, and the lecturer is a high-ranking government official of a Central American country noted for its human rights violations. The candidate's group attempts to shout down the speaker and, at one point, rushes the podium and tosses a bucket of blood at him as a symbolic protest. During the deliberations of your department, several colleagues argue that the candidate is unfit for tenure because she clearly does not respect the principles of freedom of expression upon which the academic enterprise is founded. How do you answer those colleagues?[1]

You are the chair of the Department of Communication at another midwestern university. It is the end of the semester, and a professor in your department has been teaching the first Gay and Lesbian Studies course to be offered at the University. The professor assigns the viewing (through video rental) of two films, *Desert Hearts* and *Taxi zum Klo*, as part of the final examination. The first film is a lesbian love story, with some nudity, and has an "R" rating. The second film is about gay male life in Germany and includes about three minutes of explicit sex, including a shot of one man urinating in another man's face. This film has an "X" rating. Students are asked to compare "the gendered character of the gaze" in the two films. A young woman in the class files a formal grievance with the university, and threatens to file a complaint with the state's Department of Human Rights. She file a complaint with the state's Department of Human Rights. She alleges that she asked the professor not to require the viewing of the films, since, perhaps because of an experience of childhood sexual abuse, she is troubled by viewing pornography. The professor allegedly responded by accusing her of homophobia and refused to change the assignment. Another student in the course, a member of an evangelical Christian group on campus, files a grievance because the professor has consistently attacked Christianity during the semester for its view of homosexuality. The student believes he cannot be evaluated fairly on his final project for the course, which is a paper defending the view that homosexual behavior is sinful, but homosexual orientation is not. The Dean has asked you to make a recommendation about how to deal with the grievances, and has asked you further to defend the existence of the course itself. What do you recommend?[2]

You are a professor of Philosophy at a small liberal-arts college in the South. During a class discussion of the concept of justice, the topic of affirmative action comes up. The arguments become quite heated, and at one point a white student says to a black student, "Look, how does it feel knowing that you got into this college with lower grades and test scores than a lot of the white students?" Your college has a code prohibiting "speech or other expression which is intended to insult or stigmatize an individual on the basis of their sex, race, color, handicap, religion, sexual orientation, or national and ethnic origin." After class, the black student requests that you file a formal complaint with the college against the white student. How do you respond?[3]

All three of these cases concern ethical problems commonly faced these days by college professors and administrators. Conservatives argue that such cases are the product of an overly politicized academic climate in which the teaching of the Great Books has been abandoned.[4] Radicals argue that such cases reflect the sorts of struggles that result as we attempt to create a fully multi-cultural, post-colonial university.[5] Whether we label the current crisis of higher education in terms of "political correctness" or the "backlash against multi-culturalism," it is clear that neither side in this highly polarized conflict has discussed the crisis in terms of *ethics*, and of the ethics of college teaching in particular. In fact, as I will argue in this essay, the current crisis in higher education is the predictable result of the lack of teaching of principles of ethics in the formation of college teachers. In the contemporary college or university questions of professional ethics are inevitably turned into questions of law and politics.

All three of the cases described above deal with the status of the professor as an advocate for a particular theory, method, or political position. All three require an evaluation and ranking of the virtues of tolerance, intellectual rigor, sensitivity, and objectivity. Much of the current debate about political correctness centers on the appropriateness of an advocacy role for college professors, both inside and outside the classroom. In order to advance the debate, I want to focus on one key question in this essay: "To what extent should a professor mask his or her views on controversial methodological and/or political questions in the classroom?" I will first discuss what professional codes of ethics tell us about the problem of teaching and advocacy, and then develop a utilitarian argument about the ethics of classroom controversy. I will anticipate objections to the argument from a deontological and virtue ethics standpoint, and conclude with some practical suggestions for improving moral inquiry about classroom controversy.

As Kenneth Farmer has written, the state does not recognize university teaching as a profession. That is, although university professors possess a body of highly specialized knowledge, require specialized training, and possess considerable autonomy, they are not certified or licensed in the same way in which physicians, attorneys, or even public school teachers are. Further, even if one argues that the requirement of a terminal degree for tenured or tenure-track employment of almost all college professors constitutes a form of certification, it is important to recognize, as Farmer notes, that such a requirement only refers to the professor's competence within a given academic discipline and not as a teacher.[6]

Physicians and attorneys are required to study professional ethics as part of their education, and are required to take examinations which cover ethical issues. Both professions have extensive codes of ethics which cover issues related to confidentiality, equality of treatment, and so on. The American Association of University Professors, the American Federation of Teachers, and the National Education Association all possess professional codes of ethics. Most college professors, however, do not belong to these associations. Individual colleges and universities possess faculty manuals which lay out certain ethical principles, but these are typically the product of debate over specific problems such as rules governing tenure and promotion or sexual harassment. Most statements about classroom conduct are highly abstract and uncontroversial. What reasonable person could disagree with this paragraph from the AAUP Statement on Professional Ethics?

> As a teacher, the professor encourages the free pursuit of learning in his students. He holds before them the best scholarly standards of his discipline. He demonstrates respect for the student as an individual, and adheres to his proper role as intellectual guide and counselor. He makes every reasonable effort to foster honest academic conduct and to assure that his evaluation of students reflects their true merit....He protects their academic freedom.[7]

The National Education Association's code includes two principles relevant to our present concern, when it says that the educator "1. Shall not unreasonably restrain the student from independent action in the pursuit of learning. 2. Shall not unreasonably deny the student access to varying points of view."[8]

Codes, of course, cannot prevent conflict of fundamental professional values from occurring in the classroom or the office. If we return to the cases with which I began this essay, we see such values in conflict. In the first case, that of the English professor who helped deprive a visiting politician of the right to speak, we see a tension between the professor's exercise of her political rights as a private citizen and her responsibility to uphold accepted standards of civility in academic discourse. In the second case, the alleged forced viewing of homosexual pornography, we see a tension between the professor's pursuit of the truth and the protection of the psychological well-being of his students. Courts have recognized that forced viewing of pornography in the classroom may be a form of sexual harassment. The professor also appears to be caught between his role as an advocate of gay rights and his responsibility of insuring student access to differing points of view. In the final case, the alleged racial harassment in the classroom, the professor is put in the position of weighing the free speech rights of the white student against the right of the black student to equality of treatment in the classroom. What does ethical theory have to tell us about the problems raised by these cases?

I will begin with the utilitarian ethics of John Stuart Mill, since it is Mill's perspective which is most applicable to questions of freedom of expression. Mill argues that in cases of ethical conflict the decision rule should be the principle of general utility: whatever promotes the greatest good of the greatest number. Although utilitarians differ over whether or not the principle of general utility should govern obedience to general moral rules ("rule utilitarianism") or be applied to each given case of ethical deliberation ("act utilitarianism"), the utilitarian view is distinctive in its emphasis on society rather than the individual, its secular character, and its applicability as a decision procedure in cases of conflict between moral rules.[9]

From the moral point of view of the utilitarian, freedom of speech, particularly in the classroom, has tremendous social utility. In an eloquent passage, often cited by civil libertarians, Mill writes,

> If all mankind minus one were of one opinion, mankind would be no more justified in silencing that one person than he, if he had the power, would be justified in silencing mankind....[T]he peculiar evil of silencing the expression of an opinion is that it is robbing the human race, posterity as well as the existing generation--those who dissent from the opinion, still more than those who hold it. If the opinion is right, they are deprived of the opportunity of exchanging error for truth; if wrong, they lose, what is almost as great a benefit, the clearer perception and livelier impression of truth produced by its collision with error.[10]

There are, then, two primary reasons why freedom of speech promotes general utility: minority views may very well prove to be the truth in the long run, and it is easier to see the truth more clearly when it has "collided" with error. One may add the third reason, implicit throughout *On Liberty*, that the general welfare of humans is greater under free regimes like those of England than of despotic ones like the Czar's or the Pope's. Mill recognizes only two exceptions to his principle. He writes that the regulation of private conduct by private authority may have been justifiable in the case of "small republics surrounded by powerful enemies, in constant peril of being subverted by foreign attack or internal commotion."[11] It is also justified in cases where a society is too backward to be capable of improvement "by free and equal discussion," and only obedience "to an Akbar or a Charlemagne" will work.[12]

Mill's arguments have been attacked by conservatives for undermining the sort of consensus which makes free societies possible. In the conservative view, which owes much both to Aristotelian virtue ethics and to Thomist natural law ethics, republics require self-imposed restraints on expression.[13] Radicals such as Catherine MacKinnon argue that the social utility of equality outweighs the social utility of free expression. Because forms of expression like pornography and sexual or racial slurs undermine equal participation of citizens in politics and students in academic inquiry they are more like actions than like speech, and thus must be restricted.[14] The ancestor of the current radical view of free speech, the controversial German emigré intellectual Herbert Marcuse, agrees with Mill's statement about free speech being applicable only when citizens have reached the point of being improved by democratic discussion and debate. But he argues further that lack of access to the mass media and the lack of true participatory democracy in the United States means that Mill's conditions for freedom of expression are not present.[15]

How would a utilitarian discuss the cases I outlined earlier? In the case of the gay and lesbian studies class, the utilitarian would argue that there is greater social utility in having the film assignment be required of all students. Further, the first student has the option of withdrawing from the class if she is offended by the material. The case of the second student is a greater problem. The teacher should, on the one hand, allow the full airing of "homophobic" views on utilitarian grounds. On the other hand, this principle undercuts the very idea of an advocacy-based course such as Gay and Lesbian Studies (or Women's Studies, for that matter) in the first place, since it seems by its nature to promote a single view of the ethical and political issues raised by the subject matter. Most cases of "political correctness" reported with glee by conservative journalists stem from courses like this one. A professor of this subject may very well respond that no one is obliged to present the point of view of Holocaust Revisionists in a course on the history of the Second World War; so why should those who have promoted the hatred of gay men and lesbians be allowed equal time in the classroom? It would seem, nonetheless, that the gay studies course, like the course on political philosophy, would be much improved, on utilitarian grounds, if students were allowed access to differing points of view.

One may rightly ask, however, about the problem of intimidation in settings such as this one. Although American law treats college students as adults (except for alcohol consumption), colleges and universities do not assume complete autonomy on the part of students. Curricula are prescribed, in varying degrees. Conduct is regulated, at least in residential colleges and universities, to a degree different from regular adults. Many colleges (especially small, private colleges) provide strong incentives for professors to monitor the psychological health of their students, and provide training programs to promote sensitivity to the special needs of students of color, women, and, increasingly, gay, lesbian, and bisexual students. Anyone who has taught a college class knows that there are many students who spend a great deal of time trying to find out the prejudices of the instructor and adjusting their papers and examination answers accordingly. There may be a great deal of social utility in withholding one's point of view from one's students. Otherwise, they may either be intimidated into not speaking up when they disagree, or they may simply slavishly follow whatever position seems to insure them the best grade in the course. It would appear as if, following Mill's point about audiences needing to be mature enough to follow open discussion and debate, that it would be reasonable to withhold one's own beliefs in large, introductory, general education courses, and be more explicit about one's beliefs in advanced undergraduate or graduate courses.

The problem of intimidation also emerges in the case of the professor throwing blood on the visiting speaker and in the case of the black student who feels assaulted by the comment of the student in class. One could discuss these two cases in different ways, even from within the utilitarian perspective, but it would appear that in the case of the visiting speaker the professor's actions are clearly in violation of the utilitarian principle of insuring access to differing points of view. Further, the professor's action raises considerable doubt about her commitment to academic freedom, and it may be justifiable to deny her tenure on that principle alone. The case of the black student is more complex. Presumably Mill would not include verbal harassment bordering on assault as an "idea" deserving of hearing. And yet this case is so much on the borderline between expressing personal insult and raising an important idea about the limitations of affirmative actions programs that one could argue against disciplining the student. A utilitarian might charge that speech codes like the one described in the case study tend to remove the responsibility for moral education from the professor. What could have been an opportunity for the professor to discuss the nature of ineffective political rhetoric or insensitive interpersonal communication instead becomes a legal issue. Thus far, courts have ruled against speech codes like the one invoked in this case study because they appear to have an intimidating effect upon some forms of research or classroom inquiry.[16] A definitive ruling on hate speech codes by the Supreme Court has yet to appear.

In summary, then, a utilitarian view of the problem of ethical conflicts caused by the political opinions of professors dictates an obligation to provide access to as many different points of view as possible and an obligation to withhold one's own opinion from students if they are not yet mature enough to discuss the opinion as an equal. It appears as if the social utility of hate speech codes is limited by their tendency to cut off opportunities for inquiry, however much they provide a symbolic reassurance of a "safe" climate for traditionally oppressed groups.

The argument that professors have the right to withhold information about their own beliefs from students would probably be the chief objection of a deontological theorist to the utilitarian view I have sketched. For Kant, the principal deontological theorist, the moral point of view requires rigorous adherence to universalizable principles. These principles must be adhered to regardless of their consequences. To evaluate the ethical character of an action on the basis of its consequences is always to invite the sort of rationalization that is the chief enemy of morality itself. Without universal principles, personal inclination will always triumph. A sense of duty is the best antidote to the competing desires which make up our inclinations. The best way to develop a sense of duty is to understand and follow the "categorical imperative."

Although Kant formulates this doctrine in a number of different ways, the relevant definition for our purposes is this: "Act in such a way that you treat humanity, whether in your own person or in the person of another, always at the same time as an end and never simply as a means."[17] Note that, in contrast to utilitarianism, considerations of context or audience do not appear. Ethical principles must be universalizable.

The implications for the classroom or for the political role of the professor are clear. The social dimension of the categorical imperative means that all students are to be treated with respect, as if they were rational, moral agents. One is obligated not to manipulate them in the name of higher ends. When Professor Charles Kingsfield in *The Paper Chase* hands a student a dime a large class on Contract Law and tells him to call his mother to say that there is serious doubt of his ever becoming a lawyer, this action is horrible on deontological grounds for two reasons: it does not treat the student with respect, and it is done in order to manipulate the student in question into working harder. A widely discussed book on the ethics of teaching, Parker J. Palmer's *To Know as We Are Known*, defends the practice of telling lies in the classroom in order to stimulate students to think for themselves.[18] Since one could never universalize such a practice and it violates the autonomy of the students, it cannot pass ethical muster on deontological grounds either.

One does not teach people to reason or to speak or write or interpret effectively by making decisions for them. Students themselves should be able to decide whether or not they accept the professor's point of view. As long as the professor treats opposing positions with respect, students should not be able to use the idea of intimidation as an excuse for not thinking or not speaking up in class. It is unclear how a deontological theorist might evaluate the notion of hate speech codes. Arguably, the existence of speech codes on college campuses encourages such excuse-making by creating an incentive for students to complain to administrators rather than confronting professors directly. On the other hand, the principle of respect for persons would seem to underlie the positive motivations for the creation of such codes in the first place.

The appeal of the deontological theory lies in its insistence upon respect for persons and upon rigorous self-monitoring to avoid rationalization of inclinations into moral duties. Most experienced professors, however, are likely to balk at the idea of inflexible moral rules applied regardless of the type of subject matter, institution, or student body. Some ideas provided by Aristotelian virtue ethics may help defend further the utilitarian view I developed earlier.

One who brings a perspective inspired by Aristotle's or Alasdair MacIntyre's virtue ethics to the classroom will ask a different set of questions than those we have discussed thus far. Virtue ethics would ask us to examine the kinds of stories we tell about the educational enterprise. What sorts of characters do we identify with, admire, or vilify? What sorts of virtues and vices do good and bad teachers and students exhibit? What kinds of places do we want our classrooms, departments, and institutions to be? Until we can answer these questions satisfactorily, we will not know who we are as professors or students or administrators, and the quest for rules of classroom conduct is doomed to founder on the rocks of relativism.

At first sight, it would appear that the virtue ethicist would resolve the sort of conflicts I have been discussing in this paper in a fairly straightforward fashion: paternalism is permissible, because education is the business of crafting souls. Restriction of speech and access to varying viewpoints is permissible, because one needs a minimum sense of civic virtue in order to engage in rational discussion. It may be the case, as MacIntyre writes, that we are in a moral mess because of the liberal pluralism of our educational system. We have lost the ability, as students, teachers, and citizens, to speak as if our lives can be understood as teleologically ordered unities, wholes the nature of which and the good of which we have to learn to discover, possessing "the continuity and unity of a quest."[19]

It is possible, however, as Lee Bollinger, the Dean of the University of Michigan Law School, writes, to defend tolerance and pluralism in terms of *virtue*, not merely utility. In contrast to other political and legal theorists who use the language of virtue ethics, Bollinger believes that the reason we must tolerate hate speech and other forms of communication which fall outside civilized standards is that by doing so we publicly reinforce our nation's commitment to tolerance as a value. Virtue, Aristotle said, is the product of habit. If we are tolerant in the hard cases, like that of the Nazis marching in Skokie, we develop both a thick skin and the ability to restrain the powerful temptation towards censorship that occurs in times of national stress. We do not tolerate error or promote pluralism because there is no truth, or because "you can't legislate morality," but because tolerance itself is a virtue necessary for self-government and liberal education. Tolerance is necessary for human flourishing, both in the classroom and beyond.[20]

A virtue ethics perspective on teaching, however, even in its more restrictive form, raises some very important questions about the issues and cases I have discussed in this paper. First, why do we have so few good models for effective college teaching? Second, why is so little time spent in graduate education in preparing students to teach effectively?

From a virtue ethics standpoint, the issues raised by the cases with which I began this paper can only be answered by attending to the character of the professor and the context of the institutions in question. Some professors, depending on age, academic field, perhaps even gender or race, will need to mask their own point of view in order to be heard by students. Some will need to be more outspoken. Some students will need to be spoon-fed material, while others can be treated more assertively. Some students will need to be called on the carpet for insensitivity, while others will need to be gently ignored. Only the teacher who possesses practical wisdom can answer these questions, and the answers depend very much on context. If we can come to some agreement on what educational institutions stand for, and what kinds of professors we wish to hire, we can safely ignore the bureaucratic quest to establish rules of conduct and decision procedures for classroom and departmental conflict.

I want to conclude by proposing some modest reforms in the higher education system of the United States which I believe would contribute much to elimination of the contentiousness that now governs much of national debate over higher education.

First, it is important that professors and institutions stand for something. Undergraduate students, in my experience, inevitably interpret pluralism as relativism. One is more likely to learn something from a Marxist or Thomist professor who is tolerant of other points of view than from a liberal who presents or deconstructs all points of view equally.

Second, professors have, as Gerald Graff has written, a moral responsibility to *teach the conflicts*. No ethical system can justify withholding access to competing perspectives on the texts, methods, and objects we study. A professor who finds it difficult to teach, say, the post-colonialist/liberationist view of Conrad's *Heart of Darkness* and believes it to be a great work of universal moral inquiry, has an obligation to bring in his radical colleague to class so that that point of view may be heard.[21]

Third, students and professors should be equipped with tools of oral communication and debate so that they are not intimidated by the harsh give-and-take of passionate inquiry. Current advocates of sensitivity in the classroom are right to draw our attention to the special needs of women students and students of color, but they do the dispossessed no favors when they make being offended an actionable offense.

Fourth, professors should be evaluated during tenure and promotion for their teaching ability, including their tolerance of difference in the classroom, whether that difference is based on race, gender, sexual orientation, or political orientation. Such evaluations, if conducted by peers and using democratically accountable procedures, would do much to turn questions of law into questions of professional ethics, thus providing clearer standards for what constitutes "hate speech" in the classroom. Questions about the ethics of teaching, as well as the problem of adapting scholarly findings to undergraduate audiences, should be required as part of every Ph.D. qualifying exam.

Fifth, political diversity should be added as an affirmative action category in job searches. If an economics department consists entirely of Chicago-school monetarists it can hardly do an effective job of presenting a balanced view of economic theory and policy. The addition of a Marxist or two would have a bracing effect on departmental dialogue. A Women's Studies Department would benefit greatly from the presence of a strong critic of feminism. (At the moment, in higher education, one suspects that most of the affirmative action hiring would be of Republicans, but this in turn may sensitize conservatives to the significance of group rights.)

In any case, there is no substitute for sustained moral reflection on the nature of teaching and of the university. To place the responsibility for ultimate decisions about the nature and functions of the university in the hands of politicians, bureaucrats, and attorneys is to undermine the very possibility of liberal education. That both the right and the left should now be so willing to place such decisions outside the hands of educators themselves owes much to our refusal to establish standards of professional ethics for our classrooms.

Notes

1. For a real case which raises similar issues, see the case of Barbara Foley at Northwestern University, as described in Carolyn J. Mooney, "AAUP Panel Finds That Northwestern University Acted Properly in Tenure-Denial Case," *Chronicle of Higher Education.* November 30, 1988, p. A17; and in Joseph Epstein, "A Case of Academic Freedom," *Commentary*, September 1986, pp. 37-48.

2. This case is based on incidents at the University of Minnesota in the fall of 1993 as described in Chuck Haga, "Film for 'U' Class on Gay History Spurs New Debate," *Minneapolis Star Tribune*, December 19, 1993, p. 1B.

3. This incident is fictitious. The wording of the speech code is similar to that of Stanford University as described in Charles R. Lawrence III, "If He Hollers Let Him Go: Regulating Racist Speech on Campus," in Mari Matsuda et al., *Words That Wound: Critical Race Theory, Assaultive Speech, and the First Amendment.* (Boulder, CO: Westview Press, 1993), pp. 66-67.

4. The classic statement of this position is Allan Bloom, *The Closing of the American Mind.* (New York: Basic Books, 1987).

5. See "Introduction," in Mari Matsuda et al. *Words That Wound*, p. 14.

6. Kenneth C. Farmer, "Ethical Teaching: The Teacher as Student Advocate," in Robert B. Ashmore and William C. Starr, eds., *Ethics Across the Curriculum: The Marquette Experience.* (Milwaukee, WI: Marquette University Press, 1991), p. 236.

7. American Association of University Professors Statement on Professional Ethics, reprinted in *Codes of Professional Responsibility.* Rena A. Gorlin, ed. Washington, DC: The Bureau of National Affairs, Inc., 1986, pp. 183-184.

8. "Code of Ethics of the Education Profession," reprinted in Gorlin, *Codes of Professional Responsibility*. pp. 191-192.

9. See John Stuart Mill, *Utilitarianism*. George Sher, ed. Indianapolis, IN: Hackett, 1979. My summary of the distinctive features of utilitarianism owes much to the discussion by William C. Starr, "Ethical Theory and the Teaching of Ethics," in Ashmore and Starr, *Ethics Across the Curriculum*, pp. 34-35.

10. John Stuart Mill, *On Liberty*, ed. Currin V. Shields (Indianapolis, IN: Bobbs-Merrill, 1956), p. 21.

11. Mill, *On Liberty*, p. 17.

12. Mill, *On Liberty*, p. 15.

13. See Walter Berns, *Taking the Constitution Seriously*. NY: Simon and Schuster, 1987, p. 222.

14. See Catherine MacKinnon, *Only Words*. Cambridge: Harvard University Press, 1993.

15. Herbert Marcuse, "Repressive Tolerance," in Robert Paul Wolff et al, *Critique of Pure Tolerance* (Boston: Beacon Press, 1965), pp. 86-93.

16. See *Doe v. University of Michigan*. 721 F. Supp. 852.

17. See Immanuel Kant, *Grounding of the Metaphysics of Morals*, tr. L. Ellington, (Indianapolis: Hackett, 1981), p. 36.

18. Parker J. Palmer, *To Know as We Are Known: Education as a Spiritual Journey* (San Francisco: Harper-Collins, 1993), p. 75.

19. Alasdair MacIntyre, *Three Rival Versions of Moral Enquiry* (Notre Dame, IN: University of Notre Dame Press, 1990), p. 197. I recognize that I am glossing over some very real differences between the Aristotelian and Thomist theories here.

20. Lee Bollinger, *The Tolerant Society: Freedom of Speech and Extremist Speech in America* (New York: Oxford University Press, 1986).

21. Gerald Graff, *Beyond the Culture Wars: How Teaching the Conflicts Can Revitalize American Education* (New York: W.W. Norton, 1992), pp. 25-33.

INTEGRATING ETHICS INTO INTRODUCTORY BIOLOGY

Paul R. Boehlke
Department of Science
Dr. Martin Luther College

I. Introduction

Biology enjoys high student interest probably because of its implied promise to help in understanding both self and the world in which we live. We enter the world naked without a user's manual, but one expects that basic biology should be able to come to the rescue. Biological information ought to be relevant for practical issues: for health and lifestyle. Furthermore, since the discovery of the structure of DNA in the 1950s, a knowledge explosion in genetic and molecular biology has occurred. Developments in biology and its technology have outrun all the other sciences. With this progress, however, have come questions and concerns about how and even whether this new knowledge should be used. Clearly, a higher level of general scientific knowledge is required merely to begin to understand the new ethical problems (Fletcher, 1988).

This essay will argue that the teaching of biology cannot be just a presentation of the content. We must ask questions about what it *means* to know these things. We must ask questions about the process that produces this knowledge: its values and its truth-claims. Finally, we must ask how we are going to act in view of this knowledge. The integration of ethics into biology is required for a true biological literacy.

II. Problems

Many biological educators still make strong efforts to introduce the undergraduate to the inner beauties of their academic discipline rather than to serve the needs of society (Moore, 1993). Little time is thought to be available to see how everything fits together within the discipline (Bonner, 1962), let alone to make connections to everyday life. Randy Moore (1993), the editor of *The American Biology Teacher*, recommends discipline (Bonner, 1962), let alone to make connections to everyday life. Randy Moore (1993), the editor of *The American Biology Teacher*, recommends shunning applications to life because no one really cares, claiming that true interest in biology will be fostered only by the excitement found within the discipline through problem solving and discovery. Discovery is difficult to stage for undergraduates, and problem solving may not be realistic. When departments ponder their offerings, introductory college courses are often saddled with fundamental concepts that are seen as "basic" to further study by future scientists. Many of these concepts are abstract generalizations which are laden with theory. Atoms and molecules are viewed as having the only reality (Peacocke 1985, p. 153). Never mind that few in the audience will ever take another biology class. The result is that biology and the other sciences are portrayed as something apart from the rest of the world.

Furthermore, in the doing of science there is a tendency to get at the facts and theory of a matter and avoid ethical considerations. After discovery scientists will say that they can show how something can be done, but that they are not personally responsible for how this information is used. The classic example is the invention and use of the atomic bomb during World War II. Fearing that Germany might develop this super weapon, America set up the Manhattan Project to do it first. Afterwards, many scientists who were involved had to deal with the dark success of their project when two of the devastating bombs were actually used on Japan.

Only slightly different is the situation in which many scientists are clearly motivated to help people who suffer from a biological deficiency. For example, scientists have discovered how to bioengineer the production of human growth hormone (HGH) to make it available to children whose bodies cannot produce this chemical. Without the hormone such children would not grow to full height. However, the availability of HGH has also led selfish people to try to turn their children into super athletes (Flowers 1989, p. 400). Society cannot expect science to consider all of the possible ramifications of a discovery. Even with knowledge of possible abuses of new knowledge, individual investigators might still rightly believe that the risk of abuse is justified by the possibility of greater good.

Nevertheless, the recent bestselling book and well-attended movie, *Jurassic Park*, play to the common popular reaction, dating back to Mary Shelley's *Dr. Frankenstein*, that scientists should not mess with Mother Nature. In *Jurassic Park* a project consultant laments after his bioengineered dinosaurs are out of control, "You decide that you'll control nature, and from that moment on you're in deep trouble, because you can't do it. Yet you have made systems that require that you do it. And you can't do it--and you never have--and you never will...your powers are much less than your dreams of reason would have you believe (Crichton, 1990, p. 351)."

Molecular biologist Maxine Singer, who has been concerned about ethics in biology and helped to set down the basic guidelines for genetic engineering, has pointed out that the problem is not exclusively a scientific one. "If the knowledge that is gained is misused, it is not because of science or the scientist, it is because of the same old human problems that have caused evil for eons (Flowers 1989, p. 398)."

Nevertheless, the problem remains a serious one for science and society. Many tend to accuse science, especially biology, of hubris, the supreme arrogance, that is, of usurping the role of God. When problems or conflicts occur, the hindsight of the common person may charge that science is discovering things that we would be better off not knowing. Lewis Thomas points out that the basis of this serious charge is emotional. Debates about attempting some specific project need to return to a reasoned evaluation of risks and safeguards (Thomas 1979, p. 68). The charge is important because it assumes that nature knows best. Agreement with the charge would compel ecologists to stop all attempts to manage ecosystems. Agreement would rule out any attempts to put nature back "to the way it should be" including curing diseases and raising the standard of living. Max L. Stackhouse (1991, p. 28) states that humans have obligations both to confess sins with regard to our treatment of creation and also to engage in its reconstruction. In so many cases we need to rise above nature.

Biology especially bears the burden of having presented society with a legion of difficult ethical and legal problems. The newness of the situations and lack of shared guidelines cause deep anxieties. For example, syndicated editorialist Ellen Goodman (1993) is appalled by the prospect of the new reproductive technologies. To many it seemed as if nature had set absolute limits, but now people need to look inside themselves and ask if some of these now possible things should be done. Furthermore, just because something can be done, is no reason to assume that it should be done.

III. A Mythological Image of the Scientist

While scientists rightly desire some protection from all the possible uses of their discoveries, teachers of a discipline may err in how they translate the work of individual scientists into the images presented in the classroom. According to Smolicz and Numan, scientists tend to become dehumanized when viewed through the educational process, and doing science is pictured as "a peculiarly rational, self-correcting, logical method or process for gaining knowledge (1973, p. 108)." Its whole justification lies in the power of its supposed objective and logical assault on the secrets of nature. In "school science" the scientist, then, is presented as an unbiased tester of hypotheses, open-minded, infallible and "even writing in the passive voice with the greatest impersonality." But doing science is never value-free; and science, if it is anything, is a human activity.

IV. Limiting the Field

Thomas Kuhn (1962, p. 37) pointed out that normal science functions by having a shared paradigm which prescribes the problems, methods and even the acceptable solutions. The paradigm tends to select problems which can be solved. Anything else is just not science. Textbooks serve to expound the body of accepted knowledge, define the legitimate problems and demonstrate acceptable methods for the next generation (Kuhn 1962, p. 10). They define the subject matter of the field for the scientist. The result is that the content and process of biology are taught to all with little consideration of the broader applications of what is discovered and without any considerations of the social and ethical implications. The student is then faced with a situation where questions and comments are considered to be outside the scope of the class and the discipline. Even when some discussion occurs, the teacher may feel constrained "to get back to biology." However, several educators have proposed that one of the fundamental failures of current mathematics and science education is that students are allowed little opportunity to engage in scientific or mathematical thinking applied to tasks and problems similar to those found *in daily life* (Halpern 1992, p. 118). On the other hand, critical thinking, questioning, and evaluation of data do occur when time is allowed for application of information to new, meaningful situations (Davis 1993, p. 7).

Martin Galstad wrote that we must beware a curriculum that is filled with what Alfred North Whitehead long ago called "inert ideas." "Such ideas are so rarefied that they make little or no difference to anybody because they are almost meaningless, stripped of flesh and blood and of life and action (Galstad 1984, p. 162)." Students need to be challenged to think about how the course content affects their lives. A biology course is not a collection of facts to be learned and merely returned.

Consider the young student who reported on his sex education. He had learned all of the proper terms for the parts of reproductive system; had seen sperm and eggs under the microscope; and had been told about sexually transmitted diseases, birth control, hormones, and the female cycle. He rightly concluded that something was missing: "After all that we never talked about whether we should do it or not!" Basically, the educational situation reflects the Garrison Keillor lament: "If you didn't want to go to Minneapolis, why did you get on the train?"

To teach sex education as plumbing and contraception with no reference to the adjacent issues of meaningful sex, emotional commitment, responsibilities to guard the partner from harm, and responsibilities toward possible conception is to teach far less than half a subject. If biology is going to raise the subject, it needs to allow for closure. Alfred North Whitehead wrote, "Whatever interest attaches to your subject-matter must be evoked here and now....That is the golden rule of education....The solution which I am urging, is to eradicate the fatal disconnection of subjects which kills the vitality of our modern curriculum. There is only one subject-matter for education, and that is Life in all its manifestations (1929, p. 18)."

Peter W. Stanley (1993), the president of Pomona College, suggests that especially the liberal arts colleges need to make sure that their faculties and curricula rise above the extreme forms of disciplinary specialization and involution that turn students' vision and concern away from the real world. "Because they are at heart undergraduate teaching institutions, liberal arts colleges have the opportunity to conceive their intellectual life and their educational mission more generously. Their campuses can be--and actually NEED to be--settings where scholars are rewarded for teaching across disciplinary lines, and are encouraged to enlarge vistas and suggest the connectedness of things to students in order that they might escape intellectual narrowness and parochialism: in order that they might actually use their understanding to make the world a better place."

For example, content in a general biology course is already likely to include the fact that all the eggs a female will ever have are set aside before she is born, while she is still inside her mother. A deeper understanding of the processes of development, meiosis, and the differences between the sexes in production of sex cells (gametogenesis) easily justifies the inclusion of this information in the course. Nevertheless, student reaction to the news of an aging egg supply is usually immediate. Someone asks, "Does this mean it would be better to have your children when you are young?"

What is wrong with pursuing that, and why not raise additional questions? Should scientists use tissues from fetuses for research? Brain tissue can be used to attempt the cure of Parkinson's disease. Most recently, researchers have indicated that it is possible to take the eggs from female fetuses and use them to help others have children. If we are to enable our students to cope with such problems, we should begin such consideration in classes where basic scientific information is available. Good ethics depends on good data. Questions will continue to spin off the original ones. Would the fetuses still be considered alive? Are the fetuses to be considered human? Would they feel pain?

V. Following the Implications

Biology teachers should not shrink from such exploration. A full literacy in biology must include dealing with the ethical issues that derive from it. Biology, of all the sciences, comes with big questions. For examples:

1. What is the nature of mankind? Richard Lewontin (1993), geneticist at Harvard fears that sociobiology is teaching us that we are products mainly of our genes. If we make war against our neighbor, it is because of our aggressive genes. He replies with strong arguments for the value and effects of our environment and our education. Lewontin points out that the math student of today, without superior DNA but armed with a pocket calculator, can do math problems that the math professor of yesterday could not do.

2. Closely related is whether we have free will. Do parents merely love babies because nature programs them to do so? Are our behaviors only the results of inanimate chemical reactions? The mechanistic reductionism of science can deceive students into thinking that we are not autonomous. Then why respect others?

3. Is the authority of biology beyond question or challenge? Is it not closer to the truth that science is limited and that it is symbiotically linked to society? Students need to understand both how science is done and the nature of its claim to truth. Students need to see that while the scientist may be expert, the facts of science are still value laden. They need to approach science not as cynics but certainly with a healthy skepticism. To know science, one must also know how its knowledge is gathered and accepted.

The impact of modern biology on our thinking includes much more. Briefly, here is a list of other issues in biology which have implications for how we act:

Our place in the scheme of things: equal with any other life form or crown of creation?
Could the natural law be hard wired in our DNA?
What is life? When does it begin? When does it end?
What is our sexuality? Is it a strict dichotomy or a continuum? Is homosexual behavior abnormal? What are the ethics of sexual behavior?
Abortion: new methods and new problems
Use of birth control
Artificial insemination
Surrogate pregnancy
Nonsexual reproduction
Family size
Prefertilization sex determination in humans
Sexually transmitted diseases
Privacy issues when the human genome is mapped
Genetic control and screening: a new eugenics movement?
Medical ethics
When does life begin?
When does life end?
Use of anabolic steroids
Patient care issues
Experimentation on humans, animals, and plants
Environmental ethics: Is Christianity to blame for the destruction of the environment? (White, 1967)
Privacy issues in use of computer data
Copyright and patient issues: Should life be patented? Should a person's genome be copyrighted?
Is science amoral?
Do we need a new ethics for new problems?

No claim is made that the above list is complete, but the impact of biology on society is clear and calls for a response. Undergraduate biology needs to recognize these issues and help students to deal with them.

VI. A Larger Role For The Science Educator

Some years ago, James Wandersee nicely listed the unique functions of science educators. His premise was Robert Yager's vision that the science educator functions like a dynamic membrane between science and society. Wandersee's ideal science educator (1) structures scientific knowledge for learning, (2) translates the language of science, (3) designs teaching materials and activities, (4) presents science content in a variety of ways, (5) studies how students learn, and (6) integrates the thinking, feeling and acting of the self-educating student in science classes. These six functions encourage science educators to allow students to follow the ethical implications of the new biology. Why should there be discipline barriers? Science education, especially biology education, should concern itself with values and how we act.

Joan C. Callahan (1988, p. 465-6) provides a useful framework for such considerations. In summary, she recommends the following approach to an issue: (1) generate a list of the known facts; (2) clarify the conflicting moral values and moral principles; (3) reflect on the options; (4) make and articulate your decision; (5) justify your decision; and (6) anticipate criticism and clarify the costs. This scheme is currently being used by students in the general biology class at Dr. Martin Luther College to write a paper on a bioethical issue.

What is desired is that students see the biologist as a whole person, not as the mythological, dehumanized scientist of "school science." Scientists are human beings with the same problems and concerns that we all share.

The objection comes, of course, that such concern in biology will rob science to pay for the philosophy. On the contrary, the first step in Callahan's scheme is to know the facts. One would have to have a good handle on the basic biology to be able to sort out a reasonable argument. Critical thinking would stimulate a desire for even more information, question the truth claims of the sources, analyze the way in which the data was produced, and force the students to make choices. What could be better in a science class than to take a hard look at the processes that produced the scientific knowledge?

Students need to learn that society affects the direction and content of science. Facts are valued. For example, in some preliminary studies with very small samples, investigators have reported differences in the brains of homosexuals and heterosexuals and concluded that this must be because of genetic differences. That may well be true, but why do we not hear the other possibility, that the differences might be caused by behavior? Is there not evidence that the environment and the behavior of an organism can also modify its physiology and anatomy? For example, in one study Jewel fish raised in community tanks where they can swim in schools have brain neurons that differ from those that are raised alone. Science is not immune to political correctness and other influences from society. Data is selected for its value. Observations can be affected by current beliefs. Biologists once believed that small human beings were contained inside sperm and made drawings of their microscope observations to demonstrate this as a fact. Under this theory females merely nourished the developing fetus which came from the male (Flanagan, 1962, p. 13). If the scientific theory is discarded, the facts can change. Undergraduates need to become aware of the important implications this has for the truth claims of science. Of course, this insight makes decision-making more difficult, but this is the essence of true education.

VII. Conclusion

Biology has presented society with an array of new ethical situations. Students need to be given practice in dealing with these problems. Introductory biology classes should not avoid these issues. Rather, the responsibility for a meaningful education in biology is embedded in following ideas, making connections, and coming to informed decisions.

References

Bonner, John Tyler. *The Ideas of Biology.* New York: Harper Torchbooks, 1962.

Callahan, Joan C., ed. *Ethical Issues in Professional Life.* New York: Oxford University Press, 1988.

Crichton, Michael. *Jurassic Park.* New York: Ballantine, 1990.

Davis, Thomas A. "Alternate Teaching Methods in Vertebrate Physiology Lab; Time to Stop and Learn It Again for the First Time." *Bioscene.* 1993, 19 (2), 6-10.

Flanagan, Geraldine Lux. *The First Nine Months.* New York: Simon and Schuster, 1962.

Fletcher, Joseph. *The Ethics of Genetic Control: Ending Reproductive Roulette.* Buffalo: Prometheus Books, 1988.

Flowers, Betty Sue, ed. *Bill Moyers A World Of Ideas: Conversations with Thoughtful men and Women About American Life Today and the Ideas Shaping Our Future.* New York: Doubleday, 1989.

Galstad, Martin. *Findings: Explorations in Christian Life and Learning.* Winter Haven, Florida: Haven Books, 1984.

Goodman, Ellen. "Technology Raises Inconceivable Issues." *The (New Ulm) Journal.* January 11, 1994, 4A.

Halpern, Diane F., ed. *Enhancing Thinking Skills in the Sciences and Mathematics.* Hillsdale, New Jersey: Lawrence Erlbaum Associates, Publishers, 1992.

Kegan, Robert. "Minding the Curriculum: Of Student Epistemology and Faculty Conspiracy." Andrew Garrod, ed. *Approaches to*

Moral Development: New Research and Emerging Themes. New York: Teachers College, Columbia University Press, 1993.

Kuhn, Thomas S. *The Structure of Scientific Revolutions*. Chicago: The University of Chicago Press, 1962.

Lewontin, R.C. *Biology as Ideology: The Doctrine of DNA*. Harper-Perennial, 1993.

Moore, Randy. "Let's Try Hedonism." *The American Biology Teacher* 1993, 55 (4) 196.

Peacocke, Arthur R. "A Christian 'Materialism'? Michael Shafto, ed. *How We Know*. Nobel Conference XX at Gustavus Adolphus College, San Francisco: Harper & Row, 1985.

Stackhouse, Max L. "Godly Cooking? Theological Ethics and Technological Society." *First Things*. 1991, 13 (May), 22-29.

Stanley, Peter W. essay in "An American Imperative: Higher Expectations for Higher Education: An Open Letter to Those Concerned about the American Future." Report of the Wingspread Group on Higher Education, Racine, Wisconsin: Johnson Foundation, 1993. An electronic version of the report of the Wingspread Group on Higher Education is available on INTERNET through anonymous ftp at the University of Wisconsin-Milwaukee. To locate the report, ftp to csd4.csd.uwm.edu, change directory to pub/wingspread/report.txt. If you have questions, call 414-229-6151 or send E-mail to help@csd4.csd.uwm.edu.

Smolicz, J. J. and E. E. Nunan. "The Philosophical and Sociological Foundations of Science Education: The Demythologizing of School Science." *Studies in Science Education*. 1975, 2, 101-43.

Thomas, Lewis. *The Medusa and the Snail: More Notes of a Biology Watcher*. New York: Viking Press, 1979.

Wandersee, James H. "Suppose a World Without Science Educators." *Journal of Research in Science Teaching* 1983, 20 (7), 711-712.

White Jr., Lynn. "The Historical Roots of Our Ecologic Crisis." *Science*. 1967, 155, 1203-1207.

Whitehead, Alfred North. *The Aims of Education and Other Essays.* New York: Macmillan, 1929.

Yager, Robert E. "Editorial: Defining Science Education as a Discipline." *Journal of Research in Science Teaching*. 1983, 20 (3), 261-262.

MORAL LITERACY: INTEGRATING ETHICS
AND FRESHMAN ENGLISH

Richard Doctor
Department of English
Muskegon Community College

20,000 newborns, usually children of crack-addicted mothers, are abandoned in U.S. hospitals each year. What should be done with the babies? What should be done to or for the mothers? In Rwanda, 200,000 people have died in Africa's bloodiest civil war. What can we do, if anything? Further north in the Sudan, millions face starvation. What obligation does the United States or United Nations have to intervene and at what risk to our own lives?

Hundreds of such decisions must be faced; our college graduates will soon be among the decision makers. How well equipped are they to confront such issues? In each of these quandaries the question is simple: "All things considered, what should we do?" (Benjamin and Curtis 10) (The answers, of course, are far from simple). Students must ponder this question, a succinct definition of ethics. The study of ethics, training in how to reason about moral issues, is needed in the undergraduate curriculum, and freshman composition classes can play an essential role.

That moral education is needed by all students should be obvious. We are fond of hailing every change in education as necessary to prepare students for the 21st century. Will not moral decision-making be a key skill in that world? Few would dispute the need for a computer or technological literacy requirement in general education. What may be overlooked is that one of the most powerful impacts of technology is the creation of new ethical problems or significantly new variations of old ethical dilemmas: To what extent can the right to privacy be constricted to satisfy the need for efficient, universal record keeping in health care? What criteria should be used to determine who receives and who doesn't receive outrageously costly medical treatments such as organ transplants? What formula can calculate the cost/benefit trade-offs when manufacturing processes damage the environment? The list of moral questions faced by the information industries, our health-care systems, and business in general is nearly endless. Training health-care systems, and business in general is nearly endless. Training students to understand only how technology works and how to use it ignores an essential component: how to arrive at sound moral judgments regarding the impact of technology on our lives.

One could also make a case that moral education is needed on a personal level for many undergraduates. Drug use, though apparently down from a decade ago, still permeates many campuses. Greed and selfishness shape the attitudes of many business school graduates. Students often lack basic honesty. Leslie Fishbein, associate professor of American studies at Rutgers University, recently reported the results of surveying over 6,000 undergraduates from 31 of the country's most prestigious colleges and universities and found this startling admission: 67% had cheated at least once in college, 41% on their exams, and 19% had cheated four or more times on tests (Fishbein A52). Can moral education help? Certainly there is no guarantee, anymore than taking a course in literature of the Bible will make one a Christian, or completing theater appreciation will make one an actor or actress. But knowledge is a step in the right direction; as Aristotle said in *Nicomachean Ethics*, the person who does not know what the good is and lacks the will to pursue it is a hopeless case, but the one who knows the good but lacks the will to follow it is at least salvageable and worth trying to train (296). Or as John Stuart Mill argued, "If we wish men [all humans] to practice virtue, it is worthwhile trying to make them love virtue...(qtd. in Holmes 29)." If courses in art or music appreciation can be justified, certainly efforts to instill similar attitudes toward what is moral are worth the effort.   An institution-wide commitment to moral education is needed to fully affect students' moral behavior, which is, after all, the result of many components. James R. Rest has identified four essential parts to moral behavior including moral sensitivity, the recognition of how others are affected by us; moral judgment, arriving at the best approach to a certain situation; moral choice, placing morality above mere self-interest; and moral action, carrying out our moral intentions (Rest, chapter 1). It is in the area of making moral judgments that the composition instructor can be most useful.

Freshmen arrive on our campuses with little or no preparation in making moral decisions. The dearth of moral education in the K-12 system is elucidated in William Kilpatrick's *Why Johnny Can't Tell Right from Wrong*. In the worst case, morality is literally ignored in the curriculum by schools afraid of breaching the separation of church and state. Since the Ten Commandments can't be posted on classroom walls, some conclude their principles can't be taught either. Some schools falsely claim to teach morality by building students' self-esteem, dubiously assuming children who feel good about themselves will not do bad things. Another approach is the seemingly innocuous values clarification system, commonly associated with Sidney Simon, where a student is asked to explain how he or she would behave in a certain situation and why. Teachers of this method are explicitly taught to refrain from making any judgments regarding students' opinions. Thus, if a majority of sixth to ninth graders believe rape is acceptable in certain situations (which one survey suggests they do), teachers are to do nothing to change students' views. Finally, a few schools make a commendable but misguided attempt to teach students morality by following the lead of the late Harvard psychologist, Lawrence Kohlberg, who advocated leading students to the highest of six stages of moral development by confronting them with difficult moral dilemmas and asking them to decide the appropriate course of action. The problem with this approach, aside from the pedagogical reasonableness of giving students ethical quandaries that would puzzle Socrates, is that it assumes students will make good choices without providing adequate guidance or rationale for doing so. In reality, students see such thorny ethical issues from many angles, and the net result is that most students naturally conclude all moral decisions are problematical and there is no agreement on what is right or wrong. A real danger exists of promoting ethical nihilism rather than sound moral reasoning.

A growing number of political and educational leaders, however, are reaching the same conclusion as Professor George H. Wood, coordinator of the Institute for Democracy in Education at Ohio University, who says, "Schools cannot be value-neutral" (qtd. in Salholz 26). People from as diverse viewpoints as former Education Secretary William Bennett and founder of People for the American Way, Norman Lear, are calling for a reinstatement of moral education in public schools. Organizations such as the Josephson Center for

Character Education, headquartered in Pasadena, California, and the Cambridge based Educators for Social Responsibility are piloting programs that aim to instill in our students indisputable core values such as respect for others, courage, honesty, and tolerance. Colleges and universities need to encourage such efforts and build upon them. Ethics across the curriculum programs of the type promoted by Marquette University's Center for Ethics Studies or the Christian College Consortium should be a key component of curricular changes in the '90s. English teachers can be a key part of the picture.

Freshman composition courses offer an opportunity for infusing ethics across the curriculum if for no other reason than they are almost universally required. The teaching of moral reasoning complements the aims of most writing classes: to help students become critical readers and thoughtful writers of arguments. Sound moral reasoning involves carefully considering all positions (critical reading) and being able to articulate a course of action (thoughtful arguments). If the aim of ethical instruction is to help students answer the question, "All things considered, what should we do?" the teaching of the research paper involves just those steps: the careful gathering and evaluation of evidence culminating in a reasoned proposal for a course of action. Slight modifications of most instructors' current methods of teaching can both enrich students' writing and increase their ability to reason carefully about moral issues. *What follow are specific steps that can be taken in selecting readings, assigning writing, and strengthening class discussion.*

First, English instructors should increase the number of reading selections that explicitly state ethical arguments. Readings in a typical freshman composition class are used for two purposes: to serve as models for how to write and to inspire ideas to write about. Often the most suitable models avoid discussing the morality of an issue. Common examples include an analysis of who are the homeless, or a position on whether AIDS can be transmitted by physicians, or an exploration of the death penalty and deterrence of crime. But most texts also include many articles that address the moral issues. Do we have an obligation to help homeless who are to blame for their situation? Does a physician have an obligation to treat everyone? Is the death penalty moral? Simply selecting readings that directly focus on ethical issues increases the discussion of ethics in the classroom. Composition teachers need to select texts carefully to infuse ethics into the classroom.

Teachers also need to focus discussions about these readings to the explicitly and implicitly stated ethical arguments. For example, many instructors rightfully use Martin Luther King Jr.'s "Letter from Birmingham Jail" to show student writers the importance of writing to a specific audience and gaining that audience's sympathy, for supporting arguments with pointed examples (both real-life and hypothetical), for using every day language effectively, etc....Without neglecting those purposes, more class discussion should be directed toward evaluating King's central thesis, that there is a discernible moral law which ought to be obeyed even if it conflicts with human law.

In many readings, however, the author's ethical assumptions are only implied. So, instructors must help students see the underlying ethical positions of arguments when not directly stated by the author. For example, the position of one of the leading advocates of animal rights, Peter Singer, is almost impossible to grasp without an explanation of the principles of utilitarianism. Singer believes the moral equation of determining the greatest amount of happiness for the greatest number of people should be extended to the greatest number of sentient beings, including all animal life. Without an explanation of the philosophy of John Stuart Mill and Jeremy Bentham, from whom Singer draws his conclusions about the importance of animals being able to feel pain, his argument makes little sense. Many debates, the abortion issue being a prime example, are counter productive because participants fail to recognize important assumptions the opponent may have but does not argue explicitly.

To assist students in seeing hidden ethical assumptions may seem impossible for some instructors who have had no formal training in ethics. Indeed, Edward A. Wynne and Kevin Ryan, who advocate the teaching of character, academics, and discipline in their handbook *Reclaiming Our Schools*, believe all teachers need a solid liberal arts education, a familiarity with both literary and historical moral stories and heroes, and a working knowledge of the history of Western ethical philosophy. Realistically, most composition instructors have the requisite background in literature, should have strong preparation in logical reasoning, and can supplement their knowledge of ethics in a variety of ways, most simply by doing something they're all good at-- reading. An ideal supplement is participation in a program such as the National Endowment for the Humanities sponsored ethics-across-the-curriculum seminars offered at Marquette University. Graduate course work is another option. A simple but effective shortcut is for English instructors to sit in on ethics courses taught by a colleague at their institution (and invite the colleague to sit in on the English class to increase ability to evaluate writing assignments and promote writing across the curriculum). One should not conclude that ethical reasoning is natural to everyone and requires no special expertise or training, but neither should a lack of educational background be considered an insurmountable barrier.

Turning to the actual writing assignments, composition teachers can make the subject matter of student essays directly address ethical issues. This goal is easily accomplished if students write critical responses to readings that directly address moral issues. Students inevitably confront moral issues when critically evaluating an essay about euthanasia entitled "Who Lives? Who Dies? Who Decides?" However, even when students write from personal experience, to practice a certain rhetorical mode or some other writing skill, students' thoughts can be directed toward the moral implications of their views, enriching their ideas and adding depth to their essays. For example, a fairly common assignment is to write a persuasive essay; students often respond with a "Why I Jog" or "Stay Away from Fast-Food Restaurants" sort of argument, perhaps writing with technical competence but leaving the reader unsatisfied with the depth of thought. Instead of writing "vacuous" in the paper's margins, teachers should ask students to defend a moral belief. They often come up with much more satisfactory content, such as "Why I Donate Time at the 'Feed-the-Hungry' Center" or "Cheating is Harmful to All Parties Involved."

Such assignments also allow instructors to introduce methods that ethicists historically have employed to determine right from wrong. For example, to arrive at a good subject for a persuasive essay, direct students to use Kant's Categorical Imperative (defined in several ways, but most simply, as "an action is considered moral if one would will that others act in the same manner in similar situations") to judge whether a belief is truly important and worth defending. Subjects such as "Why I Own a Poodle" when subjected to the question "Would I will that all people own poodles?" are readily seen as trivial, whereas a subject such as "Why I Don't Cheat on my Income Taxes," when subjected to the same test appears obviously worth defending.

When assigning the research paper, teachers can require students to confront moral arguments. It is easy for students to avoid ethical issues. A paper addressing the effectiveness of sex education programs in public schools could, for example, center solely on the evidence for reduced pregnancies and communicable diseases or the qualifications of trained teachers versus parents. However, it is simple to require that a key moral issue be addressed in at least part of the paper. "Does anyone ever have a right to impose his or her values on another person?" is one of several relevant moral questions in the sex education debate. It is difficult to imagine any issue of public policy that does not raise several moral issues.

If the composition course involves readings in fiction, poetry, or drama, as is often the case, introducing moral issues is almost unavoidable. If instructors choose traditional works long recognized for their literary value such as *Huckleberry Finn*, *The Scarlet Letter*, *The Grapes of Wrath* and hundreds of others, the moral issues raised are so obvious they need not be pointed out. Perhaps we do need to remember that the study of literary texts has long been recognized as an effective tool in developing good moral habits. Probably no moral indoctrination in the virtue of generosity is more effective than vicariously experiencing its power in O. Henry's "The Gift of the Magi" or seeing its opposite, Scrooge, in Dickens' *A Christmas Story*. Teachers need only take care to direct attention to the moral issues raised in the work. As Kierkegaard pointed out in *Either/Or*, aesthetic and moral values need not be mutually exclusive, but we can make them so if the focus of literary analysis is solely on the aesthetic value of a text. Students can examine the symbolism of the river in *Huckleberry Finn*, but it should not be at the expense of ignoring the numerous passages where Huck wrestles with his perceived conscience as he judges the hypocrisy of conventional morality and its accommodation of slavery. Such passages engage what psychologist Robert Coles calls the "moral imagination" (76), a faculty which he found essential in the moral development of children. The imaginative involvement of students with the lives of others, especially people very different from themselves, is often the instructor's rationale behind the selection of alternative literary texts.   If an instructor deliberately chooses non-traditional literature to promote an appreciation of our nation's cultural diversity, an extended discussion of why such texts have been chosen inevitably leads to an examination of important moral issues.

The promotion of cultural diversity raises the first of several potential problems English instructors may encounter when introducing ethical issues to a freshman composition class.   It is difficult to find a collection of readings for freshman writing courses that doesn't laud itself on being the most multi-cultural text on the market.   Whatever the virtues of promoting appreciation for diverse voices in literature may be, and there are many, one danger is, if the texts are not used carefully, that students are encouraged to become thorough moral relativists.   A central aim of such texts is to suggest there are many ways to view the human experience.   True enough, and such readings can help students recognize their hidden prejudices and unexamined moral assumptions.   Kohlberg and many others recognize the importance of questioning conventional morality as a key step in moral development.   Unfortunately, what is at least implied in most multi-cultural reading texts is the assumption that all views are equally valid. But as Boston professor William Kilpatrick points out, "To assign equal validity to all cultures, customs, and values is to create the educational equivalent of a Tower of Babel.   The result is bound to be both cultural and moral confusion" (127).   It is the moral confusion that should concern us.   By emphasizing our differences, what is over looked is the tremendous amount of common ethical ground all cultures, nations and ethnic groups actually share.   A powerful example of our commonality that students should read is the perhaps most multi-cultural text ever written: the United Nations' "Universal Declaration of Human Rights." Its   repeated   use   of   such   words   as   "the   conscience   of mankind...universal...all members of the human family...common understanding...everyone without distinction" help students see that within cultural diversity exists a great body of shared values (quoted in Ashmore 163-64). Diverse voices need to be heard; that's how we grow morally, by literally learning to extend our sympathies to an ever larger number of people. Additionally, teachers can attack ethical relativism and affirm universal common beliefs without persecuting students who believe otherwise. But students also need to learn that universalizability is a key concept in determining appropriate ethical actions, and as ethicist Robert Ashmore points out, "An inability to universalize behavior is a hallmark of amorality" (4). Advocating cultural diversity must not obscure this principle. As historian Arthur M. Schlesinger Jr. has cogently argued in *The Disuniting of America*, the moral stakes in overemphasizing the *pluribus* in *E pluribus unum* are very high, and educators must insist that "our values are not matters of whim and happenstance" (137).

If instructors can temper the subtle leanings toward ethical relativism of most reading texts, they must also be prepared to deal with the same viewpoint from students. Whatever else one may say about Professor Alan Bloom's *The Closing of the American Mind*, it would be difficult for any experienced teacher of undergraduates to deny Bloom's opening sentence: "There is one thing a professor can be absolutely certain of: almost every student entering the university believes, or says he believes, that truth is relative" (25). It may be that few students really believe in pure relativism, that there are no standards at all to judge right from wrong. Yet many will expressly advocate that perspective, either because they haven't thought very hard about what they really believe, or because it's easier to dismiss tough issues with a "Who's to judge?" remark that ends discussion. What my colleague, philosophy instructor Blair Morrissey, calls "conversation stoppers" roll easily off students' lips; such remarks as "Where do we draw the line?" and "What's right for you may not be right for me," or "This is all just a matter of opinion" can quickly end discussion of moral issues if the questions and the questioner are not confronted.

One risky but effective method to force students to examine whether they really believe there are no standards to judge right and wrong is to assign an essay and carefully articulate the standards by which it will be graded: unity, coherence, detail, focus, appropriate and correct language and so forth. Then collect the assignment and without reading the essays randomly assign grades ranging from A to D; accompany each grade with an appropriate terse remark that only suggests agreement or disagreement with the student's position: "You're absolutely, right. Great essay! A" or, "I disagree with your presuppositions, C-" and so forth. Return the papers and wait for the outrage from students that is sure to follow: "You didn't say anything about my organization!" or, "What about my excellent examples!" or, "This isn't *fair*; you said you would grade us on how well we wrote, not on whether you agreed with us or not. You didn't keep your word." Without letting students suffer too long under the delusion that the grades will actually count, the instructor can effectively point out that students do believe in something called fairness; they believe people should keep their word; they believe actions should have reasons; they believe trust should not be violated. Though some will still be reluctant to admit that there are standards by which matters should be rightfully judged, at the very least the experience will tell them that instructors are not unreasonable to ask for reasons and evidence for a position, that "conversation stoppers" do nothing to help us move toward making a decision about "All things considered, what should we do?"

Less risky is to point out gently to students that they are making statements which they probably really don't believe. When a student says, "It's always wrong to impose your values on someone else," the instructor can respond that she imposes values on the class all the time: be punctual; dishonesty will not be tolerated; offensive remarks to other students are not acceptable; and many others. Ask if these actions are wrong. Or, have the student imagine going to the local county jail or nearby state prison. Which inmates would the student unlock and allow to leave because society had wrongly imposed its values on them? If students wish to fall back on the position that "Whatever a society says is right is right for the people in that society," ask minority members of the class if slavery, once the law of the land, was moral; or ask female students if laws denying women numerous rights were just. In summary, teachers should respect students who seriously defend the position of ethical nihilism; many philosophers and other thinkers have strongly argued this viewpoint, and it is impossible to say with absolute certainty that they are wrong. But when students advocate such a position because they have not thought seriously about it, or because it's easier to stop difficult conversation with such remarks than explore an uncomfortable idea, then the instructor should intervene and help students think through their positions more clearly.

At the other end of the reasoning spectrum from the ethical relativists are students who also discourage class discussion of moral issues: the absolutists, usually religious, most often conservatively Christian. To respond to an ethical question by saying "The answer is right here in St. Paul's letter to the Ephesians, chapter five, verse..." is an equally effective conversation stopper. The easiest way to help such students is to remind them of the importance of audience. The student can be told that if he or she were writing for an audience of believers, say the local Baptist congregation, citing Scripture references would be effective and expected, but, since the audience for student papers ought to be classmates whose religious beliefs vary widely, such quotations do not constitute proof. The limits of citing authorities in moral arguments should also be discussed; quoting St. Paul should be viewed as no more or less relevant than citing Plato or Mill, and any use of authorities without detailed reasons and examples defending their positions is of limited value in defending an ethical position.

A more difficult decision instructors face is how far to challenge a student with firmly held, but perhaps unexamined, moral beliefs. Certainly the degree of trust and safety the teacher has been able to create within the classroom is a determining factor. But some challenge is necessary. Even Professor Arthur Holmes, chair of the philosophy department at the evangelical Wheaton College of Illinois, says that "Prooftexting--that common practice of citing verses piecemeal and out of context in order to make a point--is inadequate....Moral education is not a simple matter of asserting what the Bible says..." (73). He further agrees with Kohlberg that in the process of moral education "...the move to a higher stage is aided by 'cognitive dissonance,' a tension that comes from realizing that my present form of thinking cannot resolve an issue" (Holmes 20). The instructor who wishes to push the thinking of a dogmatic student best accomplishes that goal by gently forcing the student to change his or her method of supporting an argument, insisting on reasoning and supporting examples instead of "prooftexts," without necessarily challenging the actual belief of the student. Respect for student beliefs should be equal for both the relativist and the absolutist. As Ashmore points out, "The difference between customary and reflective morality, then, is not based on *what* is believed. The same tenets may be held by both. The difference turns on *why* the beliefs are held" (2). Challenging students' moral reasoning need not be accompanied by bullying their moral beliefs.

By assigning relevant readings about moral issues, creating writing assignments that force students to take ethical positions and argue them, and gently directing class discussion away from avoiding moral issues, freshman composition instructors can accomplish much in equipping students to face the difficult moral issues they will confront in their lives. But it is also essential that teachers model ethical behavior for students as part of an institution-wide commitment to teaching ethics across the curriculum. Rules, such as those against plagiarism or against using sexist or racist language, need to be explained, justified and fairly enforced. Instructor conduct must match instructor comments. If students discuss in class the importance of keeping one's word, the principle must be reenforced when students show up for posted office hours. If the grading of essays includes such standards as "thesis must be supported with reasons and evidence," then detailed explanatory comments must accompany the grades students receive. Aristotle may have been the first, but certainly not the last thinker, to observe that we learn what is right by looking at the action of good people (7). Composition teachers need to be such good people.

References

Aristotle. *Nicomachean Ethics*. Trans. Martin Ostwald. New York: Macmillan, 1962.

Ashmore, Robert B. *Building a Moral System*. Englewood Cliffs, New Jersey: Prentice-Hall, 1987.

Benjamin, Martin and Joy Curtis. *Ethics in Nursing*. New York: Oxford University Press, 1981.

Bloom, Allan. *The Closing of the American Mind*. New York: Simon and Schuster, 1987.

Coles, Robert. *The Moral Life of Children*. Boston: Atlantic Monthly Press, 1986.

Fishbein, Leslie. "Curbing Cheating and Restoring Academic Integrity." *Chronicle for Higher Education* 1 Dec. 1993: A52.

Holmes, Arthur F. *Shaping Character*. Grand Rapids, MI: William Eerdman's, 1991.

Kilpatrick, Robert. *Why Johnny Can't Tell Right from Wrong*. New York: Simon and Schuster, 1992.

Kohlberg, Lawrence. *The Philosophy of Moral Development*. New York: Harper and Row, 1981.

Salholz, Eloise, et. al. "Values in the Classroom." *Newsweek* 8 June 1992: 26-27.

Schlesinger, Arthur M. *The Disuniting of America*. New York: W.W. Norton, 1992.

Wynne, Edward A. and Kevin Ryan. *Reclaiming Our Schools*. New York: Macmillan, 1993.

CHALLENGING THE RECEPTACLE MODEL OF EDUCATION

Dorothy Engan-Barker
Department of Educational Foundations
Mankato State University

Our tutors never stop bawling into our ears,
as though they were pouring water into a funnel....
- Montaigne, 1850

For quite a long time now, polls have shown that teachers, students, and the public in general have regarded discipline issues as the number one problem in American public schools. Several studies have shown that, especially in the large urban schools, over half of the allotted student contact time is taken up with non-instructional tasks, most connected to keeping order (Sadker & Sadker, 1991). However, recent surveys of classroom teachers show that this concern has been edged out of first place and replaced by a larger dilemma--student apathy.

Everyday, in most every classroom, most every teacher meets a sea of apathetic and resistant faces which--if they spoke what they felt--might say, "How can I get through this class without thinking?" (Paul & Nosich, 1992, p. 5)

One of my graduate students, a long-time high school teacher still passionate about his profession but finding it ever more difficult, wrote despairingly, "Sometimes I think I should carry a little mirror with me to check on who among my students is still breathing."

I suppose we who are college teachers should be grateful that, by the time students reach our classrooms, only one of these problems persists. However, that is small comfort to committed faculty whose meticulously prepared "interactive projects" frequently fail to elicit enthusiasm, whose efforts to engage students in spirited debate often result in silence. At the same time, there are programs--indeed, entire educational systems--in which students voluntarily invest themselves in their own education, and, in every case, demonstrate higher levels of academic achievement and personal satisfaction. What makes the difference?

In this essay, I shall attempt to show:
1) that educational systems, at all levels in the U.S., pay homage to democratic principles in their rhetoric, but almost universally fail to model them in their practice;
2) that this failure is significantly related to problems reported by teachers, specifically, those which are concerned with student apathy, and, on a more global level, to issues of social responsibility; and
3) that teachers at all levels, including those of us who teach college students, have a moral obligation--that is, if we do subscribe to democracy--to practice what we preach.

The theoretical framework on which this paper is based is drawn primarily from the ideology of John Dewey.

Listening to History

> *The authority of those who teach is often*
> *an obstacle to those who want to learn*
> *- Cicero*

Probably there has never been some golden age of education when students clamored for knowledge, and teachers, as Montaigne would have them do, only served to "clear the way" for their charges' voluntary forward motion. We seem rather to have adopted, along with his curricular suggestions, Aristotle's notion that, in order to produce the "good man and citizen" as well as maintain a "single society of freemen and peers...[t]he young must learn to obey a free government of which they will eventually be members; and in doing so they will also be learning to govern when their turn comes" (Aristotle, p. 314). It is true that Aristotle allowed no room for his teacher to model anything but the life of a virtuous human being, and he made clear that those in power must not govern in the interest of the governors but of the governed. However, his demand for compliance to a system of education "which may seem more appropriate to a government of slaves" than to that of "freemen," has strong implications for our present society where the education of the next generation still depends on a system of "youth enslavement"--albeit temporary--and its rewards continue to be distributed more closely along lines of social class than on meritocracy.

Furthermore, the idea of passive, compliant receptacles evolving, through some process of spontaneous generation, into an active, responsible citizenry not only flies in the face of what we now know about learning theory (for example, regardless of their preparation program, the overwhelming majority of teachers tend to teach as they were taught), but even contradicts Aristotle's own views expressed later on: "Experience is always needed, in every sphere of activity, for judging rightly the results attained; for understanding intelligently the means and methods by which they are attained; and for seeing which of them harmonizes with which" (Aristotle, p. 358). In viewing the need for good legislators, he points out that "Sophists offer to teach, but none of them practices the science he teaches...and we do not find that they have ever succeeded in turning their sons or any of their friends into statesmen" (Aristotle, p. 357).

Perhaps the greatest challenge to the receptacle model of education was launched by John Dewey. Before the turn of this century, when Dewey was planning for the laboratory school which he began on the University of Chicago campus, he looked about for desks and chairs which seemed suitable for the type of education he envisioned for children.

We had a great deal of difficulty finding what we needed, and finally one dealer, more intelligent than the rest, made this remark: "I am afraid we have not what you want. You want something at which the children may work; these are all for listening." That tells the story of the traditional education (*The School and Society*, p. 31).

Things may have changed considerably at the elementary level since then, but certainly at the secondary and post-secondary levels, nearly all classrooms are based on the listening theory--or the receptacle model. This practice continues, even though plenty of research, as I shall point out later, tells us that the most effective learning, at any level, takes place when students are actively engaged in the process of learning, i.e., the questioning, the analysis, the creation of new knowledge--as *they, themselves, choose to construct it.*

Dewey calls the traditional classroom interchange a place where the student shows off to the teacher and the other children the amount of information he has succeeded in assimilating from the textbook. "[I]t may safely be said that when a teacher has to rely upon a series of dictated directions, it is just because the child has no image of his own of what is to be done or why it is to be done. Instead, therefore, of gaining power of control by conforming to directions, he is really losing it--made dependent upon an external source" (*The School and Society*, p. 130)

Thus far, the challenge to the receptacle model rests primarily on the need to motivate learners so they will learn more. It makes good sense to embrace a practice which not only helps students but makes our lives, as teachers, more pleasant. What is important to emphasize in this discussion is the ideology which drove Dewey's words and actions. Underlying his insistence on recognizing and developing the self-determining abilities of students was his belief that only this could provide the citizenry needed for a healthy, democratic state. Democracy, he declared, must be born anew with each generation, and education must serve as its midwife. Every classroom, he believed, must function as a microcosm of the society which is most worthy of being modeled--i.e., a democracy--so that students, when adult, will have both the knowledge and the experience necessary to assume the civic responsibilities required to nurture and uphold that society.

Quite simply, Dewey's calls for change in the classroom, while not ignoring teachers as authority figures and the need for students to "learn obedience," grew from his belief of what was needed to maintain and further the collective social good. A curriculum promoting student-centered, real-life activities was merely the vehicle.

The school is fundamentally an institution erected by society to do a certain work, to exercise a certain specific function in maintaining the life and advancing the welfare of society. The Educational system which does not recognize that this fact entails upon it an ethical responsibility is derelict and a defaulter....[H]ow many who speak glowingly of the large services of the public schools to a democracy of free and self-reliant men affect a cynical and even vehement opposition to the "self-government of schools!" These would not have the [students] learn to govern themselves and one another, but would have the masters rule them, ignoring the fact that this common practice...may be a foundation for that evil condition in society where the citizens are arbitrarily ruled by political bosses....Moreover, the society of which the [student] is to be a member is, in the United States, a democratic and progressive society. The [student] must be educated for leadership as well as for obedience. He must have power of self-direction and power of directing others, power of administration, ability to assume positions of responsibility....The school cannot be a preparation for social life excepting as it reproduces, within itself, typical conditions of social life (*Moral Principles in Education*, pp. ix, 7, 10).

Unfortunately, the vehicle carrying Dewey's vision, i.e., focusing on the methods which capture children's interest while ignoring the moral basis from which those methods derived, came to have a life of its own, with little connection to its ideological underpinnings.

The Unheard Voices

Socrates, and later Arcesilaus, first had their disciples speak,
and then they spoke to them.
- Montaigne

Dewey's ideas, along with those of other Progressivists, have made an indelible impression on U.S. educational systems. But, much to Dewey's own dismay, this impact was felt primarily in the arena of instructional technique where students continue to be done to and for, however much there may be "hands-on" activities. There is little to indicate that the hierarchic power structure has weakened in terms of opportunities for increased student decision-making, with its corollary, student accountability. (Perhaps the recent trend of calling teachers by their first names can be viewed as a concession to "equalization" processes.)

Theodore Sizer, in his preface to the 1992 edition of *Horace's Compromise*, paints an unforgettable picture of what nearly all of us have experienced, but which, only in retrospect, we see in its grotesque reality. He speaks of the "senselessness of the [school] regimens" and what it must be like to

> change subjects abruptly every hour, to be talked at incessantly, to be asked to sit still for long periods, to be endlessly tested and measured against others, to be moved around in cohorts by people who really do not know who you are, to be denied any civility like a coffee break and asked to eat lunch in twenty-three minutes, to be rarely trusted, and to repeat the same regimen with virtually no variation for week after week, year after year....They [the students] make do, make their treaties, make their compromises. They assume that this is what they are supposed to do: this is Going to School in America....And as a result, there is all too often no edge to their thinking, no deep habits of intellectual interest, little curiosity beyond the immediate. Even in elite schools they have been cheated, and they don't know it. The exceptions among them, the academic or athletic tyros who are regularly heralded by their communities, prove the rule. The unspecial majority cheerfully mark time (p. xi).

It is my perception that many students do not so "cheerfully mark time." There is a growing resemblance of school to the prison model: locked classroom doors, guards on patrol in the halls, restroom monitors, metal and weapon detectors at building entrances, and required passes for every conceivable activity, including the use of restrooms, with the time required for this function carefully recorded.

An international study carried out in the 1980s by the Office for Economic Development and Cooperation (OECD) discovered that fourteen- and fifteen-year-olds, regardless of class or culture, experience school as an isolated world in which their own beliefs hold little importance. Their descriptions referred to school as "a holding tank," or as a place "where no one cares what *you* think." My own research in a blue-collar suburban high school revealed that students perceived their own academic success or failure as being largely a function of "whether the teacher can teach me or not."

These conditions should be of concern to us as college instructors if for no other reason than that students accustomed to some or all of these restrictions are entering our classrooms. And I am not sure we are doing much to alter their perceptions of "how things ought to be." Certainly much in our students' college life resembles Sizer's description above. We continue to perpetuate a model which almost ensures that students, though liberated from many of the public school restrictions, will remain comfortably in their passive roles. And, as I shall discuss later, attempts to break out of this paradigm can create painful experiences for everyone concerned. Students learn early on that their school success is largely determined by how well they carry out directions as prescribed by the adult in charge and this provides an easy transition to the next step--holding the teacher responsible for how well or how poorly they do in a course.

The receptacle model relies on a system that says teachers do and students are done to. Whatever one may say about teachers' authority deriving from knowledge differential, the fact remains that universities continue to prescribe specific coursework, as opposed to identifying outcomes which students can attempt to meet on their own terms, thereby bringing us students who are "forced" to attend our classes ("Look, I wouldn't even be here but its a required course in my major.") And teachers continue to dole out grades on which student "success" rests, much as I relied on M & Ms when my children were too little to understand other reasons for doing something worthwhile. It is almost inevitable that attention to "what the teacher wants" and "getting the grade" will supercede the desire to learn something new and interesting. Even when material might be engaging and spark some interest, twelve years of socialization as a passive learner seem to act as a barrier to this spark being fanned into a full-blown fire for learning.

James Coleman and Torsten Husen, in *Becoming Adult in A Changing Society* (1985), refer to the present relationship between adolescents and the adult world as a "socially induced irresponsibility" and suggest that this period "largely coincides with the early period of post-secondary education." I agree with their appraisal, but totally disagree with their proposed solution. "Unlike elementary school and secondary school, and unlike later work life, there are no penalties for being absent from daily activities, nor penalties for being late. There are no continuing demands for performance, but only occasional assessments through examinations" (p. 59).

I would argue that the condition they describe is not a result of the absence of imposed penalties, but rather the proliferation of such activities throughout the twelve or thirteen years in which they were developing into adults.

> From the psychological standpoint it may safely be said that when a teacher has to rely upon a series of dictated directions, it is just because the [student] has no image of his own of what is to be done or why it is to be done. Instead, therefore, of gaining power of control by conforming to directions, he is really losing it--made dependent upon an external source" (*The School and Society*, p. 130).

Rather than trying to change this condition, we, at the college level, often make concessions to it by continuing the very practices which maintain the socially induced irresponsibility we claim to disdain.

It seems we are trying to address an educational, and thus societal, dilemma without implicating ourselves. A colleague who teaches in a school of medicine tells his students that, to understand how a complex organism works, one does not study the action of just one or two of its parts, even though they may be the parts that are dysfunctional, but how they all work together, examining how each impacts the overall system. This is essentially how philosopher Gary Fenstermacher would have us view the complex organism of *learning*. He suggests that we must first change our language to more accurately reflect what really goes on in classroom interactions. It is true, he says, that what teachers do in classrooms can be called *teaching*. But what students do should be described not as *learning*, but as *studenting*. What happens in the sphere where these two activities are taking place can rightfully be called *learning*--whether or not the learning is intended or unintended, or even connected to the *teaching* topic. *Learning* simply implies that, as in any interdependent organism, every element within the sphere is affected in one way or another, and influences every other element's functioning.

> Every relationship in life is, as it were, a *tacit or expressed contract with others*, committing one, by the simple fact that he occupies that relationship, to a corresponding mode of action (Dewey, *Ethics*, p. 312)

The ways in which we teach probably have little to do with our respective content areas or even with trends in instructional methodologies. In addition to Latin verbs or algebraic formulae, students learn from us, their teachers, what we believe about ourselves, about them, and about the educational enterprise. How we teach is, more than anything else, a reflection of our belief systems. Observe four different teachers of history, for example, and one is apt to see four different modes of instruction. We tend to refer to these as "teaching styles" as if they are a function of personality types. That probably plays a part, but a more authentic explanation must acknowledge that our teaching practices result primarily from our beliefs about what a teacher "ought to do and be" and, the natural corollary, what we perceive as the "appropriate" role of students.

I shall further argue that all teachers, not just those who happen to be in teacher education programs, must consider with renewed seriousness Dewey's charge regarding the Sisyphean nature of democracy's birth and examine what our role as midwives demands of us. If we really believe in democratic principles, which, according to George Bernard Shaw, ensures that a nation gets exactly the kind of governing it deserves, then we are ethically bound to model that belief not only in our rhetoric but by our actions in the classroom.

About Rights and Freedoms

*It may be that we no longer know how to create the kinds of situations
in which persons are likely to choose themselves as committed and as free...*
                                   Maxine Greene, Dialectic of Freedom

In seeking examples where there have been efforts to challenge the
receptacle model in education, it is necessary to look primarily at
research done in K-12 schools. Little is available at the post-secondary
level.

Literature on school effectiveness shows that those schools which
actively involve students in *authentic* decision-making processes have
fewer problems with discipline and truancy (Edmonds, 1979). This
holds true regardless of setting--urban or rural, large or small. The
decision-making processes in which schools involve students must be
real and important to the effective operation of the school--as in
scheduling programs and developing behavior codes, not contrived--as
in selecting prom themes or choosing class colors. Furthermore, they
must embody real consequences for which students are held
accountable, insofar as such accountability is appropriate. In a more
recent study, Mary Ann Horenstein (1993) visited twelve Blue Ribbon
secondary schools, from Maine to California, which had been identified
for their effectiveness. She discovered that, above all, each has a vision
of how a school "ought to be" and, *in each school, both teachers and
students are empowered and have a voice in the decisions that concern
them.*

At the college/university level, considerable research has been done
on factors affecting student retention and academic success. One
important factor is *internal locus of control* and how the degree to which
students possess this affects their success in college work. A few studies
link this to instructional methods, i.e., describing practices which might
foster greater internal locus of control for students, but none that I
know of discusses the issue in terms of its ethical implications for
teachers, or its implications for contributing to a larger good than that
of the individual student.

In colleges of education, of course, "active learning" theories comprise a large part of Methods coursework. The emphasis, however, is almost entirely on aspects of curriculum development, selection of textbooks and resources, and techniques for instruction. The broader ramifications, or their relationship to ethical practice are, at best, taken to be implicit assumptions or, as seems to be more often the case simply not seen as relevant. Apart from my own (still incomplete) studies and those being carried by a colleague in our department, I have uncovered essentially no research done with college students in the specific area of "democratic pedagogy."

"Doing Democracy"

Only as it is lived can it be learned
- William Kilpatrick

In our department, all of us have complained of the difficulty in generating rousing classroom discussions where students really seem to care about the outcomes. We have met to discuss textbooks, curriculum, and our own instructional strategies. Over the past year, a colleague of mine has conducted an experiment in his classes in which students are asked to determine characteristics of educational systems in totalitarian nations. Participants consistently identify similar elements:

"[D]evelop students to accept and to do what they are told, not to think for themselves, not to question, and to be passive...." Participants are asked to raise their hands if they believe a major part of their educational experience has been as the one they described for their dictatorial system. Nearly all hands are raised, every time (Bussler, 1994, p. 1).

Rene Hersrud, also of our department, reports that there is some evidence to indicate that

students who actively participate in the discussion and resolution of problems at classroom, school and community levels are more likely to participate in the democratic process as adults and to develop more accurate social perceptions which ground their thinking about the social and political environment (1991, p. 22).

While much of what passed as Progressive Education towards the middle of this century did not bear much resemblance to Dewey's dream of the democratic classroom, the "Eight Year Study," conducted by the Progressive Education Association during the 1930s, provides us with the most substantive work done in attempts to assess the effectiveness of Deweyan ideology applied to the classroom. The study, carried out over eight years, compared the college performance of almost 3,000 high school graduates from traditional and progressive schools. It is likely that the small difference between groups in academic achievement--progressive school graduates earned slightly higher grades and slightly more academic honors--accounts somewhat for the little mention made of the study later. What seems at least as important is that progressive school graduates, during their college years:
- were judged to be more objective and precise thinkers
- were judged to possess higher intellectual curiosity and drive
- were more resourceful
- participated more frequently in the arts and in student groups
- demonstrated a more active concern in world events (Sadker & Sadker, 1991, p. 292-3)

While one must take care in drawing unwarranted conclusions, we might ask what would happen if college and university teachers discontinued the practice of connecting success in coursework to satisfying a teacher-determined list of criteria, (e.g., no more than two absences, at least 20 points on each essay and a minimum of 75% on the midterm and final exams) and, instead, required students not only to help set criteria for assessing mastery of expected outcomes, but provide self-evaluations of their own progress toward a mutually agreed upon goal. Would the subject matter acquire some meaning beyond its ability to show up in credit form on a transcript? When identifying goals and objectives for course syllabi, do we seriously address process outcomes?

Faculty in my field of social, philosophical and psychological foundations of education have initiated efforts to make democratic process a visible and integral part of our classes, identifying it as a course goal along with content objectives. For example, "Expected Outcome III" in the syllabus for my undergraduate course, "School and Society," reads, "Students will be able to work effectively within a democratic classroom process, demonstrating respect for self and others, and a commitment to building community."

Over the past three quarters, I have attempted to establish in my own teaching some guidelines that will help me break out of the controller mode and wean students from the receptacle model they are accustomed to. Things do not always work as I envision in the planning process, but as a result of trial and error and feedback from colleagues, the following elements seem most critical to success:

1. Challenging the receptacle model has everything to do with process, little or nothing to do with content. Courses with many sections and a common textbook, as in our "School and Society" course, offer no obstacle to dramatically altering ways in which content outcomes can be achieved.

*I had the same text as my roommate did last quarter, but we did
entirely different things with it. (P.S. Our way was better--once I
got used to it--and I'm sure I learned more.)*

2. Outcomes must be clearly defined. Presumably we do know what it is within our own realm that is most worthwhile exploring, but considerable decision making should be left up to students to determine processes used in meeting the outcomes and how they will demonstrate mastery of those. Some expected outcomes leave little room for options (...*writing which reflects knowledge of composition skills, including correct spelling, grammar, and punctuation*). Others give considerable latitude for student creativity (...*evidence of critical thinking processes*).

3. We need to tell (and tell and tell) our students why we so prominently include process outcomes as course goals. This goes beyond reciting research about increasing their achievement or sense of control. We need to use the *language* which identifies the ethical

dimension in which our practice is grounded: *democratic process, social responsibility, professional integrity.*

> *This class is the first time I've thought of democracy as something outside the voting-booth-majority-rules sort of thing.*

Naming our behavior partially addresses Kilpatrick's charge made over fifty years ago, "...[D]emocracy is a faith not yet thoroughly accepted, a hope as yet only partially justified, and a program that largely remains to be made. What is thus lacking exactly defines our duty" (cited by Bussler, 1994, 2).

4. Group work is central to meeting the goal of establishing a community of learners. There must be clearly defined expectations and regular in-class projects which automatically require individual accountability.

> *I studied a lot more than I usually would [for a group exam], knowing that my group members grades were dependent on me doing my share.*

Of course, there are those who do let their groups down, but it then becomes a dilemma which the group must confront and solve, rather than a game between teacher and student. Attendance problems are significantly reduced.

> *It's the first time in three years of college that I didn't blow off as many sessions as I dared--it was sort of like never missing football practice, even when you didn't feel like going.*

5. De-emphasis on grades and emphasis on student self-evaluation is essential. Strangely enough, most of us can pretty accurately assess our own performance in nearly anything. We know if we have done a decent dive, an acceptable somersault, or sewn a straight seam. It is only in the realm of "studies" that students seem not to have a clue about the quality of their work. I think we can lay this almost entirely to the fact that students have nearly no say in how to construct their

own knowledge. One of my students says he still remembers the "D" he received in sixth grade on a paper he spent two weeks writing. They had been studying mythology and he decided to use Superman as his mythical figure. His teacher not only found this unacceptable but joked about it in class.

I have also found it remarkable that students have a consistent tendency to evaluate their work at a lower level than it actually is. (Or perhaps that is a phenomenon that occurs only in the self-effacing midwestern psyche). At any rate, it is always gratifying, to both teacher and pupil, for me to be able to say, "Kerry, you are underestimating yourself!"

> *I never knew I could do the kind of work I did in here. I really* _do_ *have something to say!*

As professors, it seems our greatest task lies not so much in expecting students to "say something," but in providing an arena in which they become convinced that they already do and should have something worthwhile to say.

Freeing Students: The (Dubious) Rewards

In response to this major investment on our part to "free" students, surely one can expect that they, in turn, have risen up and called us blessed. Would that it were so. The quotations above attest to some successes. However, my colleagues and I have discovered the meaning in Dewey's warning:

> Familiarity breeds contempt, but it also breeds something like affection. We get used to the chains we wear, and we miss them when removed. 'Tis an old story that through custom we finally embrace what at first wore a hideous mien. Unpleasant, because meaningless, activities may get agreeable if long enough persisted in. *It is possible for the mind to develop interest in a routine or mechanical procedure if conditions are continually supplied which demand that mode of operation and*

*preclude any other sort....*Yes, that is the worst of it; the mind, shut out from worthy employ and missing the taste of adequate performance, comes down to the level of that which is left to it to know and do, and perforce takes an interest in a cabined and cramped experience. (*The Child and the Curriculum*, p. 27-28).

What we have discovered is that our efforts to democratize the classroom are not always embraced by our students. They are, in fact, often resented. As implied earlier, students' success often relies on a heavy dose of teacher behavior which can only be characterized, at best, as caring paternalism and, at worst, dictatorial. When that is removed, it is obvious that "clearing the way" for students can mean clearing the way for failure as well as for success. (Perhaps this is related to philosopher Arturo Fallico's admonition that teachers must never stand in the way of a student's "healthy existentialist crisis!") In spite of the fact that far more planning and preparation must be devoted to this form of instruction, it is not always recognized by students.

I felt as if I was expected to do the professor's job.

If she isn't willing to teach and tell us what we should do, how did she get this job in the first place? My dad is a teacher and he says the most important thing you need to know about teaching is making sure the students know who's boss--whether its kindergarten or college."

At the other end, there are a few students who experience a sort of transformation.

This course changed not only the way I look at my classes, but at my life. I guess, at some level, I always knew that what I learn and get out of college is up to me, but I see myself as having more power in other ways as well--which can be good or bad, because now I feel guilty when I don't work for some of the things I say I believe in.

Faculty in our department enjoy consistently positive feedback from students. However, if we are honest, we would have to admit that, after their first experience with our *democratic process* objectives, many view it with mixed feelings.

I understand what you're trying to do with this "democratic process" stuff, and I guess we need to do it--especially since most of us plain to become teachers--but it sure can be painful!

Changing the Paradigm or Can One Find Meaning in a College Classroom?

The world without its relationship to human activity is less than a world.
- John Dewey

People who teach in colleges and universities have been accused of living in an ivory tower, a place where knowledge is collected, organized, divided up, and disseminated by people who justify its value through "remote reference[s] to some possible living to be done in the future" (*The School and Society*). Students, it seems, have no problem accepting this view. Their frequent references to "when I get back into the real world" suggest that they see themselves as temporarily in exile, traveling through a make-believe land only long enough to acquire the passport necessary for passage back to reality.

It is not that meaning and relevance are absent in college classrooms. But it is necessary to question the way in which we approach the task of "teaching meaning." Indeed, there is renewed emphasis on the teacher's role in "character development." Especially in my own discipline, literature abounds. No less a personage than R. Freeman Butts has issued a poignant call for "the meaning of citizenship in a democratic society [to] become a central theme in all liberal education and in all teacher education" (1993, p. 329). He goes on to cite an impressive list of scholars from Berkeley, Princeton, Northwestern and other places, who "have been reinvigorating the concepts of democratic citizenship in liberal education...." He makes a compelling case for "leadership in our colleges and universities that will encourage the liberal arts faculties as well as school of education faculties to unite" in making civic education central at all educational levels. He lauds the work being done by the Center for Civic Education and the Council for the Advancement of Citizenship:

> The genius of CIVITAS is that it deliberately seeks to define the meaning of citizenship in American democracy and outlines the civic values, the civic knowledge, and the civic skills that American citizens need to possess in order to live up to the ideals of democratic constitutional government...[it] drew upon leading scholars from history, political science, political philosophy, law, and other social sciences and humanities as well as from experienced professionals in education and public service who hold a broad range of political, economic and social views. It outlines in detail the values fundamental to the civic virtue, the common core of civic knowledge and skills, and the civic participation that are necessary to achieve [good citizenship]....Let us concentrate on making civic education a regular, recognizable and prominent part of the curriculum, the life and the culture of all educational institutions from elementary to graduate school (p. 331-333).

My own graduate study in the history of education began and ended with works by Butts. Now long retired but still producing books and journal articles, he is described by the editors of one journal as "the quintessential foundations professor." But after reading his latest piece, I was reminded of the poster I once saw in a small, ill-appointed Salvation Army booth: "I was hungry so you formed a committee to study my problem." In all the rhetoric, I still see little that requires us, the teachers asked to "teach" these lofty ideals to the next generation, to examine our classroom practices using those ideals as the measuring rod. I expect, given the current emphasis on the issue and the unspoken assumption that it will ease the ills of a violence-prone society, that we shall feel increasing pressure to "teach ethics" in our colleges and universities. Our own university system is looking at adopting an ethics requirement for graduation. Indeed, perhaps many of us are already bravely lecturing to our students about these very issues and, to ensure that they are learning what they need to know about "civic responsibility," are demanding that they write, in 10-12 pages, thoughtful, critical final papers worth 40% of their grade.

I suspect Camus got it right when he said, "for an idea to change the world, it must first change the life of the one who holds it."

References

Aristotle. *The Politics of Aristotle.* Ernest Barker, ed., tr. London: Oxford University Press, 1958.

Bussler, D. "The Democratic Class: Social Infrastructure Developing Social Architects." *Teacher Education Quarterly* (publication and copyright pending).

Butts, R.F. (1993) "The Time is Now: To Frame the Civic Foundations of Teacher Education." *Journal of Teacher Education.* V. 44, No. 5. 326-334.

Coleman, J. & Husen, T. (1985) *Becoming Adult in a Changing Society.* Paris/Washington, D.C.: Organization for Economic Cooperation and Development (OECD).

Dewey, J. (1899/1956) *The School and Society.* Chicago: The University of Chicago Press.

-----. (1902/1956) *The Child and the Curriculum.* Chicago: The University of Chicago Press.

-----. (1909/1959) *Democracy and Education.* New York: Macmillan.

Edmunds, R. (1979) "Effective Schools for the Urban Poor." *Educational Leadership.* (37), 15-24.

Fenstermacher, G. (1978) "A Philosophical Consideration of Recent Research on Teacher Effectiveness." *Review of Research in Education.* 6.

Greene, M. (1988) *The Dialectic of Freedom.* New York: Teachers College Press.

Horenstein, M. (1993) *Twelve Schools That Succeed.* Bloomington, IN: Phi Delta Kappa.

Hersrud, R. (1991) "The New Social Studies: Vision or Reality for Elementary Curriculum?" Unpublished manuscript.

Sadker, M. & Sadker, D. (1991) *Teachers, Schools and Society*, 2nd Ed. New York: McGraw-Hill.

Sizer, T. (1984/1992) *Horace's Compromise: The Dilemma of the American High School*. Boston: Houghton Mifflin.

WEAVING ETHICAL THREADS INTO THE NURSING CURRICULUM FABRIC

Patricia Finder-Stone
School of Nursing
Northeast Wisconsin Technical College

INTRODUCTION

Hardly a day goes by that a nursing instructor is not involved in knotty discussions with nursing students about ethical dilemmas which they have confronted in the clinical area. What should they have done? How could they have performed more competently or compassionately? What are the right answers?

In the high-technology health-care system of today, it is essential that nursing students be prepared to guide clients and their families through the tangle of ethical complexities in their search for reasoned decisions.

Curtin (1978) says that nurses must identify, clarify, and organize their thoughts about ethics and nursing. She states "Nursing is vitally concerned with ethics because nursing is essentially a moral act! That is, its primary moral conviction shapes its fundamental nature. Its basic concern is with the welfare of other humans, and its technical skills are developed and designed to that moral end."

It behooves the nursing instructor to point out the need for basic understanding of ethical theory early in the educational program along with brief discussions of everyday ethical concerns faced by nurses. Because ordinary dilemmas which are a part of routine nursing practice are so "ordinary," instructors must focus students' attention upon them or they may not be recognized. If beginning students can gain solid ethical foundations early in their nursing education by analyzing and reflecting about controversial issues, they will become better prepared to deal with the incredible complexities of the very powerful dilemmas into which they may be plunged in the course of their clinical assignments.

STATEMENT OF THE PROBLEM

Nursing, historically, has been described as a "doing" profession. Many students correlate their personal progress in a nursing program by how skilled they might be in giving injections, starting intravenous infusions, distinguishing heart murmurs, or reading EKG strips. It is doubtful that a discussion of ethical theorists would be identified as a top priority by the student upon entry into the program.

Therefore, constructing a framework for ethical decision-making for highly focused students who are intent on skill mastery and procedural techniques requires not only a sense of timing but also a commitment from the faculty to prepare the nurse for the twenty-first century appropriately.

A review of the literature (e.g. Parsons, 1988; Husted, 1991; Brady, 1981; Curtin, 1978; Curtis, 1986; Aroskar, 1980; Wright, 1987) presents many common components upon which ethical decision-making frameworks may be based.   Such elements include identifying or clarifying the problem or dilemma, gathering and analyzing data, understanding of ethical theory, addressing personal values, selecting a course of action based upon ethical principles and reflecting upon one's own and others' reasoning.

In order to address these components in an adequate manner in tightly-packed nursing curricula, it is necessary that nurse educators develop a coherent plan.   Although the writer approaches these concerns from a technical/community college perspective, it is suggested that the model can be applied in diverse undergraduate educational settings.   A suggested sequence follows:

- Reflections on personal values (values clarification)
- The ANA Code for Nurses with interpretive statements
- Introduction to ethical theory
- Overview of ethical principles:
    respect for persons/autonomy
    nonmaleficence/beneficence
    justice/distribution of scarce resources

veracity/trust
- Implementation of ethical reasoning

REFLECTIONS ON PERSONAL VALUES

Most students enter nursing to help others, and the personal values which they bring with them will have profound impact upon their practice--how they perform as a nurse. Certainly the clearer they are about what they value, the more congruent will be their actions with their beliefs. Thus, it would seem that nursing students' awareness of their personal value systems through classroom discussions related to the valuing process as well as their use of the Values Clarification Process (Raths, et al., 1966) could be an appropriate beginning. Examples of published exercises to aid in this process can be found in *Values Clarification in Nursing* by Steele and Harmon (1983). These activities can provide an avenue for personal growth and ethical reflection, even though the research is sparse to indicate that participation in the process leads to more effective ethical responses when students are confronted with dilemmas. The nurse educator can encourage students to reflect upon their behavior as well as the actions which are expressions of their values. Such introspection may help learners discover inconsistencies in their personal value systems which could lead them first to gain deeper self-understanding, followed by an increased understanding of those for whom they care.

THE ANA CODE FOR NURSES

Following this reflection upon personal values, it is proposed that students now turn to their professional values.

The American Nurse Association Ethical Code for Nurses (ANA, 1985) is the official statement of the national professional nurses' organization for the United States. Developed in 1950, and revised on a regular basis since that time, it is the foundation for ethical decisions in professional practice. It serves to inform the nurse and society of the profession's expectations and requirements in ethical problems. Its basic stance stresses accountability to the client. Its purpose is the promotion of human rights and ethical responsibility in the profession of nursing. When students learn that an integral function of the Code is that of encouraging ethics and human rights content in basic, graduate, and continuing nursing education, they may be better able to see its relevance.

After reflection upon their personal values, aspiring nurses should be urged to examine the underlying principle of the code, respect for persons, as to the personal and professional implications for them. Consider the statement, "Neither physician's prescriptions nor the employing agency's policies relieves the nurse of ethical or legal accountability for actions taken or judgments made." Could a nurse be discharged for refusing to accept an assignment to the intensive care unit (ICU) if she had not practiced in the ICU setting for many years and felt the assignment constituted unsafe practice? Could she be terminated for this ethical stance? Should she accept the assignment even though she feels inadequately prepared? Would the other ICU nurses focus less on their critically ill clients in order to help her as a float nurse? Would she be left flounder in this unfamiliar setting? Questions such as these frequently arise in the clinical setting with no easy answers.

The ANA Code requirements often exceed those of the law. That is, one may perform ethically, but still be subject to civil or criminal liability. Now students will have to ask themselves what it really means to be a nurse. Does that nurse who is asked to report to ICU feel more obligated to the client whom he/she does not know than to the institution in which she practices? What would the student do as this practicing RN? On what grounds?

ETHICAL THEORY

In order to answer questions such as those presented in the previous section, the student needs background in ethical theory. According to Mappes (1991), "An ethical theory provides an ordered set of moral standards...that is to be used in assessing what is morally right and what is morally wrong regarding human action in general." Murphy (1983) notes, "Nursing's association with the humanities has been a fleeting one at best, and the baccalaureate student gets it out of the way in the first two years of her education so that she can then be educated to function in a technological environment." And technical college education, historically, offers little to no opportunity to gain humanistic insight into its technical occupations. Therefore, it is imperative that nursing educators focus some attention, albeit briefly, on the major ethical theories commonly involved in health care decision making. Starr (1991) stresses that a systematic theory can only be effective if it is consistent and practical.

There is no single way to address the complex issues of ethical theories in a health care context, and comprehensive discussion is beyond the scope of this paper. However, it would be helpful for students to be introduced to the subdivisions of deontology and teleology and be able to differentiate between them in order to consider alternatives in ethical decision making.

Teleological (from the Greek, *telos*, meaning "end") theories determine actions to be right or wrong according to the consequences of those actions. That which is right is generally a function of that which is good to cherish, according to teleological theory. The most prominent teleological theory is utilitarianism, represented by John Stuart Mill (Sher, 1979) who is best understood as seeking "the greatest possible balance of value over disvalue for all persons who would be affected." The two major approaches which should be presented to students are act-utilitarianism, that is, judging single actions for long term consequences, and rule-utilitarianism, which proposes adherence to certain moral rules upon which everyone in society is obligated to act. As applications are universalized, exemptions to those applications must also be universalized.

The limitations to teleological theory can also be discussed with students. For example, quantifying relative good and harm of actions seems close to impossible, especially in relationship to health care issues. Focus upon maximum happiness, good, or value tends to ignore the rights of the individual. Yet, *most health care decisions seem to be based upon the utilitarian model.*

The second subdivision which the nurse educator should present is that of deontology (from the Greek, *deon*, meaning "duty"). Deontology attempts to identify what is right or wrong based upon duty or obligation rather than upon what the consequences of an act may be. The most prominent of classical deontological theories was developed by Immanuel Kant, who formulated the condition of the Categorical Imperative, which asserts that all people should be respected and treated as ends rather than as means to an end. Because of *its emphasis upon duty and obligation to other persons*, this writer suggests this theory should be of maximum importance in ethical decision making in nursing practice.

Detailed discussions of these and other theories should be recommended for students to explore according to their time and interest. It is imperative for the instructor to stress that in-depth study of these complex philosophical theories will enhance their ability to engage in rational discourse with colleagues as well as peers from other disciplines. However, such discussion is beyond the scope of this chapter.

OVERVIEW OF ETHICAL PRINCIPLES

After students have struggled with the theoretical foundations of ethical decision making, they will next need to identify basic principles and then reflect on their usefulness to help provide that analytic framework to which this writer has previously alluded. Again, students need to be reminded that there are no easy answers. Knowledge and discussion of basic ethical principles will not necessarily produce resolution of ethical dilemmas. As students engage in dialogue, they will identify which principles are more securely grounded than others in specific situations.

This writer believes the fundamental principle for nursing practice, the principle that underlies all other principles relating to nursing practice, is that of respect for persons. Respect for persons entails the recognition of the unconditional worth of each individual in our human society. Nursing students early on are encouraged to develop the art of empathetic understanding: using the clients' frame of reference; viewing situations from their perspectives; accepting clients without passing judgment. This respect for individual dignity is commonly referred to as the principle of client autonomy, that is, the right of self-determination. Nursing students will need to consider potential infringements upon client autonomy as they look at the many components of autonomy. For example, the poor pregnant woman who has chosen what she considers her only alternative in a given situation, abortion, may find her autonomy is limited because public funding will not pay for the procedure. The critically ill motorcycle accident victim on a ventilator may not be able to articulate his choices for treatment because he has been intubated. The client who has been diagnosed with prostate cancer may agree to undergo a radical prostatectomy with the associated complications if he has not been informed about the current effectiveness of radiation therapy treatment. Perhaps the option of no treatment at all has never been presented. Unless this client is given full information regarding risks and benefits of treatment, autonomy is seriously limited. When the client who has experienced a cardiac arrest in surgery is resuscitated in spite of the do-not-resuscitate (DNR) order on his chart, his self-determined choice is not being respected. What is the nurse's professional role when he or she confronts situations where the client's autonomy is limited or ignored? How can the nurse take into account respect for client autonomy without infringing upon the autonomy of colleagues? Who decides?

As the instructor guides the student through issues of autonomy and informed consent, discussion should also address concepts of competence, or decision making capacity, ability to understand the consequences of decisions, and the type and amount of information which is to be shared.

It is certain that such issues will not be decided in an undergraduate classroom, but the dialogue which these issues produce can assist the nursing student to develop a stronger sense of self. As stated by Fowler, "An interplay between the principle of respect for persons and the duty to respect autonomy and the human dignity of the patient suggests that there is a partial foundation in nursing for the kind of contract relationship based upon superior moral standards rather than consequentialistic outcomes" (1987, p. 47). Even commonly confronted situations regarding disagreements between client and family members or care providers about treatment and care can place ethical principles related to autonomy at stake.

The case presentation of the request of Elizabeth Bouvia (Annas, 1984), (a multiple sclerosis victim whose autonomous choice for termination of feedings conflicted with caregivers professional responsibilities) is an excellent reference for the principle of autonomy as well as its limitations. It provides fertile ground for students to delve into the ethical dilemmas related to professional nursing.

A discussion of the principle of autonomy frequently precedes those of beneficence and nonmaleficence. There may indeed be a tension between respecting personal freedom of the client or pursuing what one may perceive as the client's best interest. The general principle of beneficence states one ought to do good or promote good, while nonmaleficence is the duty to do no harm.

Frankena (1973) interprets four separate meanings of the principle of beneficence: "1) one ought not to inflict evil and harm; 2) one ought to prevent evil and harm; 3) one ought to remove evil or harm; and, 4) one ought to do or promote good." What, then, is good? When does doing good become causing harm?

The ability to preserve life through artificial feeding can usually provoke vigorous discussion among nursing students as they reflect upon beneficence and nonmaleficence. For some, preservation of life must be balanced against the sanctity of life. Beginning students need to be reminded that nutrition and hydration do not mean just "spooning in chicken soup" but actually involve procedures which can increase risks of infection, aspiration pneumonia, or restraint, thereby keeping the client alive but possibly in a somewhat captive state. Discussions of the proportionality of possible benefit as opposed to a disproportionate burden can help students keep an open mind on these controversial issues.

Instructors can refer students to the American Nurses Association Position Statements and Guidelines which state that acceptance or refusal of food or fluid should usually be respected, because competent adults are generally in the best position to evaluate harms and benefits to themselves in their own personal contexts. This ethical judgment is well established legally (Nelson, 1986) through various cases affirming the right of competent persons to refuse treatment, including food and fluid. Yet the issue repeats itself on a regular basis in clinical practice. It is important, however, that students be cautioned to guard against indifference or misplaced respect for client autonomy without determining the client's reasons for refusal, as those reasons established the right and are pivotal in determining nursing actions.

In addition to considering the morality of highly publicized cases related to beneficence and nonmaleficence, nurses, in their role as client advocates, must learn to alleviate suffering associated with painful procedures and must also demonstrate the ability to maintain an environment for quality nursing care. Because the definition of nursing clearly states that the practice of nursing is the diagnosis and treatment of human response to actual and potential health problems, the opportunities to "do good" through the promotion and restoration of health are unlimited. Even the tremendous increase in the number and kinds of pharmacologic preparations can present an ethical challenge for nurses, as they must develop and maintain high levels of alertness for side effects which could cause more harm than benefit to their client.

A major issue confronting our nation at the time of this writing is that of the distribution of health care. How do we allocate resources in an ethical manner? What is just? For example, successes which we have had in the development of ultrasophisticated technologies have kept many people marginally alive, but also have escalated costs, produced increasing demands, and created unprecedented ethical and economical dilemmas. What is a just way to determine allocation of resources? Equal sharing of resources does not address problems of scarcity. Entitlement theories of justice do not address the issue of needs. A justice as fairness theory gives little weight to individual autonomy or problems of paternalism. Even allocation according to needs is problematical when we see the need to decide between conflicting needs.

We could have discussions about the controversial development of the artificial heart or the overuse of magnetic resonance imaging (MRI) or computerized axial tomography (CAT) techniques, but beginning nurses may fail to see a relevance to themselves. They may, however, make appropriate connections about justice when they need to prioritize their own nursing care. Should they spend more time with their AIDS client, who at this time is desperately in need of psychosocial care, or should the semi-conscious individual with the central infusion line, chest tubes, and apprehensive relatives be their immediate priority? Consideration and reflection over such issues which may arise in their own practice may help them clarify their philosophy of care when they extrapolate to the whole of society.

The principle of veracity (truthtelling) is essential in the nurse-client relationship. In the past, a paternalistic (maternalistic) conception of the provider-patient relationship seemed to support a policy of untruthfulness. When disclosing information to help clients understand their illness and treatment, nurses will be held to the reasonable standard, that is, what reasonable or prudent nurses would disclose under the same or similar circumstances. Nursing students will learn that openness in communication and care are complementary. Most people know that fresh air and sunshine can give remarkable assistance to the healing process. In like manner, the openness of truth is integral to good nursing care.

In today's society, in order to function with rationality, clients must have access to the truth about their condition because truth is the basis of trust. Once lying and deception occur, truth is eroded, but with truth, trust flourishes. Truth telling can provide nurses with a practical way to direct their values into a logical reasoned response.

Situations for discussion might include those cases where nursing staff are asked to participate in deceptive practices such as withholding truth regarding a client's diagnosis or prognosis, questionable practices of placebo administration, or, perhaps more perplexing, sharing one's status as an HIV-infected caregiver with the client. Discussion and reflection upon issues such as these will help to guide the students' actions in ethical decision making.

THE ETHICAL REASONING PROCESS

Limitations of time in the basic nursing curriculum do not allow the luxury of extended philosophical argument about ethical dilemmas. Nurses must be prepared to make quick decisions and be accountable for them. Using an appropriate method of decision making can help to provide nursing students with a basic structure for thoughtful consideration of dilemmas which they may encounter in their practice.

The foundation of nursing practice is the nursing process, a systematic problem-solving model to provide individualized care for clients. This nursing process which is familiar to nursing students can be extrapolated to the decision making process when addressing ethical dilemmas, as they both share several common characteristics. Both processes require analysis of the situation and action under conditions of uncertainty. Limitations of time and space preclude discussion of the nursing process, but all basic nursing textbooks cover this unifying concept of nursing in depth.

An approach which may be used in the ethical decision making process follows:

Identifying the Problem
The first step in ethical decision making is the recognition or perception that an ethical problem or problems exist. The nurse may experience a conflict of duties, a conflict of personal or professional values, or even, perhaps, an ethical code violation by a colleague.

Collecting and Analyzing Relevant Data
The nurse will need to examine the ethical context, that is, what precipitated the problem. Who are the major players/participants and decision-makers (the client? family members? health care professionals? others?) and what are their interests and viewpoints

in this situation?

Clarifying the Ethical Problem

Now the nurse will correlate principles from the ANA Code of Ethics for Nurses as well as other ethical principles to determine whether or not they give adequate direction for action. It may be necessary to prioritize them if several issues are involved. The nurse must continue to be aware of personal responses to maintain clarity in problem solving.

Identifying and Weighting Possible Alternatives

Once the nurse has a clear perception of the ethical problem, a list of options for action can be formulated which will both maintain the client's rights and the nurse's professional integrity. Construction and review of arguments weighing all sides would follow. If appropriate the nurse may decide to use institutional assistance such as ethics committees, pastoral care, etc., for counsel.

Selecting and Implementing for Action

After evaluating the alternatives, the nurse will implement the plan that maintains consistency with his or her own moral norms.

Evaluating the Outcome

Reflecting upon the outcome may help the nurse assess personal or moral feelings about the whole situation. Consideration should be given to modification of the current plan if indicated. Hopefully, the nurse will identify ways a similar dilemma may be avoided in the future.

CONCLUSION

The socialization of nursing students into ethical professional practice is an ongoing process. This paper presents one suggested pattern for introducing ethical dialogue into the beginning level nursing courses. Concepts can be added and developed as the student progresses to the more challenging clinical area where the dilemmas increase in complexity, variety, and particularity.

Reflection upon personal and professional values and ethical theories and principles may help nursing students answer "What should I do?" Doing what is good or right will not come automatically.

Answers are not necessarily black or white, but may be many shades of gray. Ethical nursing practice will not come about just by thinking or discussing abstract concepts. Rather, it is the integration of those concepts into ethical behavior that is the mark of the truly ethical nurse.

References

American Nurses Association. "Code for Nurses with Interpretive Statements." American Nurses Association, Kansas City, MO, 1985.

Annas, G. "When Suicide Prevention Becomes Brutality: The Case of Elizabeth Bouvia." *Hastings Center Report*, 1984. vol. 14, p. 20.

Aroskar, M. "Anatomy of an Ethical Dilemma." *American Journal of Nursing*, 1980. vol. 80, pp. 658-660.

Brody, H. *Ethical Decisions in Medicine*. Boston: Little, Brown and Company, 1981.

Curtin, L. "A Proposed Model for Critical Ethical Analysis." *Nursing Forum*, 1978. vol. 17, pp. 12-17.

Curtis, B. *Ethics in Nursing*. New York: Oxford Univerity Press, 1986.

Fowler, M. & J. Levine-Ariff. *Ethics at the Bedside*. Philadelphia: J. B. Lippincott, 1987.

Frankena, W. *Ethics* (Second Edition). Englewood Cliffs, NJ: Prentice-Hall, 1973.

Husted, G. & J. Husted. *Ethical Decision Making in Nursing*. St. Louis, MO: Mosby-Yearbook, 1991.

Mappes, T. & J. Zembaty. *Biomedical Ethics* (Third Edition). New York, NY: McGraw-Hill, 1991.

Nelson, L. J. "The Law, Professional Responsibility, and Decisions to Forego Treatment." *Quality Review Bulletin*. Joint Commission on Accreditation of Hospitals. January, 1986.

Parsons, A. & P. Parsons. *Health Care Ethics*. Middletown, OH: Wall & Emerson, 1986.

Raths, L., M. Harmin, & S. Simon. *Values and Teaching.* Columbus, OH: Charles E. Merrill Books, 1966.

Sher, G., ed. *Utilitarianism* by John Stuart Mill. Indianapolis, IN: Hackett Publishing, 1979.

Starr, William C., "Teaching of Ethics." Robert B. Ashmore & William Starr, eds. *Ethics Across the Curriculum: The Marquette Experience.* Milwaukee, WI: Marquette University Press, 1991.

Steel, S. & V. Harmon. *Values Clarification in Nursing* (Second Edition). Norwalk, CT: Appleton-Century-Croft, 1983.

Wright, R. *Human Values in Health Care.* New York, NY: McGraw-Hill, 1987.

BUSINESS ETHICS AND WHITE COLLAR CRIME: BLUEPRINT FOR AN INTERDISCIPLINARY COURSE

William J. Maakestad
College of Business
Western Illinois University

INTRODUCTION: Why This Course?

Since at least the mid-1970s Colleges of Business in the U.S. have been engaged in a debate over how best to integrate ethics into their curricula. One recurring issue is whether ethics study should be (a) concentrated into a single course, or (b) integrated by each department throughout the curriculum. The debate has yet to be resolved, either by consensus or by the major accrediting body for the nation's leading business programs, the American Assembly of Collegiate Schools of Business (AACSB).

The debate has been healthy, but too often business ethics education is still compromised. For example, in my AACSB-accredited program, faculty college-wide are "encouraged" to introduce ethical content into their courses. In reality, however, business ethics receives extensive, systematic attention in but a single introductory course, "Management and Society," only an elective for most business majors. The COB currently utilizes no faculty from the Department of Philosophy, and the business faculty who teach this course have strong interest, but no special training, in moral philosophy and ethics. There are many reasons for the absence of a full-scale commitment to ethics education, a common phenomenon among business programs nationwide. Yet certainly one of the most important reasons is the continuing perception among many business faculty that ethics education is a "soft value" that must give way to the "hard skill" demands of the competitive marketplace.

Outside the academy, the social consequences of the increased attention given to ethical violations and criminal liability for corporations and their executives since the 1980s has been profound. For instance, both the incidence and visibility of white collar prosecutions increased dramatically during the 1980s. According to the

American Bar Association, in 1970 the number of corporate and white collar cases accounted for barely eight percent of all federal criminal prosecutions, but by 1985 it had risen to a quarter of all federal prosecutions, a 300-plus percent increase. In the meantime, cottage industries of ethics consultants and white collar defense lawyers have emerged to assist business in picking up the pieces following ethical and legal lapses by management.

Yet, university curricula have continued to be slow to respond to these developments. After informally surveying a significant number of business programs around the country, for example, I discovered not a single course that specifically explored the moral goals of the criminal law *vis-a-vis* society's increasing ethical demands of business. Ultimately, by not being informed of the higher ethical and legal standards now being applied in this changed business climate, students who enter the workforce unaware are often the ones who pay the consequences--as, of course, does our society.

This article describes my modest attempt to address this vacuum by developing a course on "Business Ethics and White Collar Crime," which was offered for the first time during the Fall 1993 term. I first summarize the course development project's objectives and innovations, expected outcomes, and plan of action. I next provide an overview of the developed course's learning objectives, pedagogical approach, and substantive content. I conclude with a brief evaluation of some of the successes and disappointments of the course as it was offered.

PROJECT PLANNING AND DEVELOPMENT

<u>PLANNED PROJECT OBJECTIVES AND INNOVATIONS</u>

My primary objective was *not* to develop yet another introductory business ethics course, but to develop an interdisciplinary seminar which would explore the relationship between business ethics and white collar crime. The course would be open not only to undergraduate business majors, but to law enforcement and liberal arts students as well. To help interest and reach such a diverse group of students, I decided to integrate business and legal experts nationwide into the course through regularly scheduled, student-led speakerphone interviews. (With permission from each interviewee, the interviews were recorded for use in future classes.) Over the course of a decade's work in the field of corporate and white collar crime, I have developed a strong commitment to introducing students to the linkage between personal ethics, corporate social responsibility, and the ends of the law. Having also developed working relationships with some of the country's foremost experts in the field of corporate crime, I felt that it was time to garner their expertise for the benefit of my students. Thus, I envisioned this course as an experiment in interactively sharing with students not only my own ideas, but those of acknowledged experts across the country.

Secondary objectives for this project included: (1) successful application(s) for internal/external grant support, which would provide release time to develop the course and the telecommunication technology required to offer the course as designed; (2) presentation of a conference paper, and publication of a journal article or book chapter, on the planning, development, and assessment of the course; and (3) presentation of a non-credit workshop utilizing my institution's new satellite uplink capability to be received by identified downlink sites, which could be at high schools as well as other colleges and universities.

My course proposal sought to build upon the strengths of two of my university's most successful academic programs--the College of Business and Department of Law Enforcement Administration--to develop what may be the first course of its kind in the country. Designed to provide students with a truly interdisciplinary perspective on business crime and ethics, the course also sought to bridge the often sizable gap between ivory tower ideals and business world realities by allowing students the opportunity to interact with national experts from the "real" worlds of law and business.

EXPECTED OUTCOMES

Beyond offering students a unique educational experience, I felt that this course presented me with challenges in the areas of instructional technique and research activity.

Instructional Technique

My course anticipated benefits reaching beyond those normally associated with interdisciplinary team-teaching, such as the integration as opposed to compartimentalization of knowledge for students, and academic stimulation and renewal for faculty. It was also designed to address directly a common complaint concerning my university's rural isolation by means of a simple, inexpensive way of bringing national experts "live" into the classroom. My single previous experience (in a graduate class) with student-led speakerphone interviews was successful beyond all expectations, and I saw no reason why it could not work in an undergraduate setting as well. I could imagine very few students who would not appreciate an opportunity to question leading authorities on the kind of professional, ethical, and legal matters they might face after graduation.

The key, of course, is preparation, which in this context means at least four things: (1) carefully selecting and assigning reading materials in the expert's field, in order to provide students with enough background to give them the knowledge and confidence to prepare good questions; (2) pooling and coordinating student questions before the interview, to weed out inappropriate or redundant queries; (3) providing the class with some basic interview techniques and rules of etiquette, and having them practice them in a mock interview setting; and (4) providing a common "touchtone" reading, which would be read by students and the interviewee.

The course also presented the opportunity to try out at least one other instructional technique to which I had recently been introduced: a practical, seven-step approach to ethical analysis in business cases developed by the influential Arthur Anderson Business Ethics Program in St. Charles, Illinois. I have found it advantageous for students to use a consistent framework for their case analyses (both oral and written) throughout the semester, and the Anderson model is flexible enough to incorporate principles I had been introduced to during my NEH-sponsored "Ethics Across the Curriculum" study at Marquette University.

The Anderson analytical model for business ethics issues requires the moral agent(s) to address each of the following questions before deciding on a course of action:

1. What are the important facts?
2. What are the ethical issues at the systemic, organizational, and/or individual levels?
3. What are the action alternatives?
4. Who are the primary stakeholders?
5. What are the ethics of each alternative?
6. What are the practical constraints?
7. What action should be taken, and why?

Because my institution had participated in a special training program offered by Arthur Anderson, I also had access to their excellent support materials, including a wide range of videotapes on ethical issues and education. For someone like myself whose primary field is not moral philosophy, these materials were especially helpful. The students likewise found them interesting and effective.

<u>Research Activity</u>

In addition to presenting a paper to at least one academic conference where I might receive peer feedback, I planned to submit for publication an article or chapter based on my experience with the course. Each would address the most important pedagogical and course content decisions I faced during both the course's development and implementation. I viewed this as a particularly interesting challenge for me, since all of my published articles to date have dealt with substantive legal issues rather than pedagogy. Preparation of such an article or chapter could also be done with an eye toward eventually seeking external grant support for furthering ethics curriculum development in my College of Business.

FROM THE BEGINNING: PLANNING THE COURSE, STEP-BY-STEP

My first task was to put together a general plan and timetable for accomplishing my project goals. I came up with the following twelve steps, which were more or less adhered to during the year I developed the course:

Step 1:   Receive permission from department chair and college dean to offer this type of experimental course. (Fall 1992)

Step 2:   Prepare and submit two small grant applications for course development support, one to my university and the other to the American Bar Association. [Both were eventually awarded.] (Winter 1992-93)

Step 3:   Meet with department chairs from business, law enforcement, and sociology/criminology to discuss optimal course scheduling and to work out cross-listing details. (Winter 1992-93)

Step 4:   Review existing resources and do preliminary research on additional course materials. Obtain commitments from two on-campus colleagues to offer guest lectures: one, an experienced research librarian, would run a practical workshop for my students on researching ethical and legal issues on business; the other, a writer and expert on the Exxon Valdez disaster, would present a class on that incident. [Both agreed.] (Winter 1992-93)

Step 5:   Plan, research, and organize substantive course materials. My second summer of NEH-sponsored

ethics study at Marquette University was especially helpful during this stage.
(Spring/Summer 1993)

Step 6:   Purchase best available speakerphone equipment with recording capability. Coordinate classroom installation with the COB Dean's office and WESTEL, the university department responsible for on-campus telephone operations.
(Summer 1993)

Step 7:   Request interviews with five national experts, with initial contact by letter and follow-up by phone. [The first five experts invited happily accepted.] Tentatively schedule interviews approximately every three weeks during the 15 week semester. Select readings and cases to be read by both students and experts were to be sent to the experts at least one week prior to interview.
(Summer 1993)

Step 8:   Organize and review final course materials and schedule; produce syllabus.
(Summer 1993)

Step 9:   Offer course. (Fall 1993)

Step 10:   Conduct extensive student course evaluations.
(Fall 1993)

Step 11:   Prepare and submit conference paper, journal article, and/or book chapter addressing issues concerning course development and implementation.
(Winter/Spring 1994)

Step 12:   Study feasibility of reoffering course as developed and/or offering revised course over Western Illinois' satellite uplink capability.
(Summer 1994)

THE DEVELOPED COURSE

COURSE OBJECTIVES

The general objectives for the course I developed can perhaps best be expressed as they were on my syllabus:

Whereas morality has to do with sets of standards which address the rightness or wrongness of conduct, ethics means reflection upon, studying and developing reasonable moral standards by which to live life in all of its environments--including on-the-job. The ancient Greeks, who were the first to struggle in a systematic way with moral philosophy, considered ethics the most practical of all subjects, because it deals with a fundamental question every thinking person asks: What does it mean to live a good life, or to be a good person? This course will provide an introduction to ethical reasoning, especially as it may be applied in business contexts. It is neither my purpose nor desire to indoctrinate students with my moral values. Rather, we will explore ways of systematically approaching moral dilemmas, with the hope that through study, practice, and discussion, we will learn from the wisdom of the past and discover that not all ways of resolving such dilemmas are equal.

We will also examine when, how and why law-- especially criminal law--is used to influence business organizations and their managerial agents. In order to effectively address the momentous legal and social changes that have pushed corporate crime issues into the public consciousness in recent years, course materials will be interdisciplinary. We will explore a rich variety of legal, historical, philosophical, and social science resources, which will allow for a deeper appreciation of the substantive, structural, and cultural components of corporate responsibility in the United

States. Special emphasis will be placed on examining issues pertaining to the health and safety of workers, consumers, and communities, and on finding positive alternatives for businesses seeking to be both competitive and moral.

Pedagogical Approach

I am convinced that one of the most effective ways of teaching moral virtue is through storytelling and metaphor. This is something that I sensed intuitively before I began my formal ethics study during the summer of 1992, and I became even more convinced after reading excerpts from philosopher Mark Johnson's fascinating book *Moral Imagination*. As a result, I decided to incorporate into the course not only actual cases of corporate and white collar crime, but also contrasting, positive examples of how socially responsible corporations and employees reacted when faced with similar business pressures. (The only previous time I had taught a course on corporate crime, corporate horror stories were presented relentlessly and exclusively, and I am concerned that students may have left the course even more jaded than they were coming in about the possibility of both "doing good and doing well" in business.)

I was also influenced by the approach that Harvard Professor Robert Coles takes in teaching professional ethics to graduate students in law, business, and medicine. Coles *exclusively* uses stories--short stories, novels, and poetry--to stimulate his professional students' moral sense, in courses widely considered among the most demanding yet popular offered at Harvard. I was neither equipped nor prepared to go that far, but I did supplement the actual cases I assigned with short fictional works by B. Traven and Bernard Malamud.

With enrollment capped at twenty undergraduates, I was able to offer it essentially as a seminar course. The goal was for the class to be highly interactive, with incentives provided for attendance and meaningful class contribution. (Attendance and participation counted for twenty percent of the final grade.) Approximately every other class period (the class met twice weekly) students would hand in a two-page analysis of an assigned reading and/or take a quiz. (These together counted for sixty percent of their grade.) Class discussions would normally focus on the reading assignments for that period, except on days when we screened videotapes or conducted interviews. Finally, I assigned group projects which required an extensive written analysis and oral presentation during the final week of the semester. (The group project counted for the remaining twenty percent of their grade.) There were no exams.

With class discussion playing such an integral role in the course (in contrast to the lecture classes I normally taught), I found the need to envision my primary teaching responsibilities differently. I found four guidelines, gleaned from Arthur Anderson materials, to be helpful reminders in this regard. First, *respect the value of discussion*! This means promoting a safe classroom environment and respecting the vulnerability of students who put their values on the line, as well as resisting the impulse to always provide the "teacher answer." However, this does *not* mean that "anything goes." Frequently it means requesting justification for positions that have nothing but emotion to back them up. Second, *prepare for discussion*! Unstructured discussion may easily lead to anarchy. To avoid this requires preparing questions that will lead the class toward the learning objectives and anticipating student comments and questions as much as possible. Third, *manage the discussion*! While students will--and should--resist simple moral indoctrination, some consistency in structure is helpful. This is where the basic analytical perspectives and frameworks introduced early in the class, including the Arthur Anderson model for ethical analysis, were absolutely critical. It is also helpful to carefully plan management strategies for dealing with especially quiet or hostile individuals or classes. Finally, *close the discussion*! This does not require neat closures at the end of every class, but does suggest reaching one or more points of consensus sometime during each discussion period. Class after class without any consensus or closure can lead to student frustration, and may reinforce feelings of relativism.

These guidelines helped maintain open, lively, and constructive classroom dialogue concerning the substantive content of the course, which is briefly summarized in the next section.

SUBSTANTIVE COURSE CONTENT: AN OVERVIEW

Except for the final week of class when students presented their group projects, the course was essentially divided into three components: (1) an introduction to basic moral and ethical concepts, definitions, and analytical tools/frameworks; (2) discussion of *Corporations in the Moral Community* by Peter French, Jeffrey Nesteruk, and David Risser; and (3) discussion of *Corporate Crime Under Attack: The Ford Pinto Case and Beyond* by Francis Cullen, William Maakestad, and Gray Cavender. A brief survey of the objectives and highlights of each component follows, with a special emphasis on the contributions of the guest lecturers and speakerphone interviewees who helped make the course truly interdisciplinary.

Introduction: Before a single business issue was ever discussed, I spent approximately one month introducing students to basic concepts pertaining to moral philosophy and ethical analysis. I began with an excerpt from Hunter Lewis' book, *A Question of Values*, which started students thinking about just how important the moral values we choose to live by are, and explored some of the ways we choose and justify the values we live by. I then assigned two short stories rich in characters who were struggling with cultural as well as moral conflicts: B. Traven's "Assembly Line" and Bernard Malamud's "The Bill." My objective in assigning and discussing these particular stories was to begin to gently move students away from the extreme moral and cultural relativism that I find so prevalent today. We then discussed a short excerpt by Joan Callahan which distinguished between morality and law, morality and economics, morality and personal taste, and morality and religion. I then lectured briefly on Lawrence Kohlberg's stages of moral development for the sole purpose of arguing that cognitive changes can and do--but do not necessarily--occur in our moral beliefs and systems.

Students were next assigned readings by Patricia Werhane and Thomas Donaldson which compared and contrasted utilitarian, deontological (both Kantian and Rawlsian), and virtue (or human nature) ethics. After leading class discussions of these philosophical approaches, I introduced the first analytical tools specifically geared toward business: stakeholder analysis (which considers the interest of every individual, group or thing affected by a business decision) and multi-level analysis (which examines ethical dilemmas through organizational and systemic perspectives as well as from an individual's lens). Next, the seven-step Arthur Anderson model of ethical analysis was introduced, along with our initial case studies.

The first month concluded with the students' initial interview. The person interviewed was a successful business owner who also serves on the board of directors of two major corporations. He was chosen because of his personal integrity and reputation for thinking broadly about the social responsibilities of business. The touchstone reading for the students and the interviewee was Albert Carr's classic business-as-poker article, "Is Business Bluffing Ethical?" As expected, the article made for interesting dialogue, especially since the businessman spoke frankly about his moral misgivings as well as triumphs, and steered clear of rank moralizing.

Corporations in the Moral Community

Each of the seven chapters in this slim volume explore in some way the moral responsibilities of modern business corporations and those who make decisions on their behalf: managers, employees, shareholders, and directors. The authors begin the book by creating a fictional corporation, Liberty Oil, which is undergoing a major crisis and several smaller ones. The major crisis is an off-shore oil spill, which is obviously modelled after the Exxon Valdez disaster. Other issues with moral implications the company faces include plant relocation, employee downsizing, and charitable contribution decisions. Characters from every level within the corporation are also introduced, each of whom will face at least one ethical dilemma by the end of the book.

It is an effective opening chapter and an exciting pedagogical tool, as references to the company and its stakeholders recur throughout the book. As the class progressed through subsequent chapters on the collective moral responsibility of corporations and the individual moral responsibility of corporate decision-makers, I occasionally supplemented the text with readings and videos to provide a new context for some of the issues raised by the authors. For example, when a Liberty Oil employee was faced with a whistleblowing dilemma, students also read an article by Sisella Bok and viewed a privately taped lecture by Roger Boisjoly, one of two engineers who blew the whistle on Morton Thiokol following the Challenger spaceflight disaster. And to further explore issues surrounding the fiduciary relationship between the directors and shareholders of a corporation, we screened an excellent PBS video entitled "Anatomy of a Corporate Takeover."

During this five-week component of the course there was one phone interviewee and one guest lecturer, each of whom contributed an interdisciplinary perspective. The interview was with the prosecuting attorney who successfully brought the first "corporate murder" charges in U.S. history against executives who caused an employee's death through knowingly maintaining unsafe working conditions. Students prepared by studying the case and asking questions not only about legal issues, but also about the moral significance of charging an employer with a crime rather than a worker's compensation claim. The interview coincided with a chapter that discussed the occasional dissonance between the legal and moral duties of employees and managers.

The guest lecturer was a poet who had studied and written extensively on the massive Exxon Valdez oil spill. With the authors modelling Liberty Oil's (its fictional corporation) troubles so closely after Exxon's, it seemed only appropriate to delve into the real circumstances and costs of one of the best known corporate debacles of the past decade. The poet's lecture was augmented by his personal collection of slides, and his humanistic presentation effectively portrayed the hidden, lingering costs of that environmental disaster.

Corporate Crime Under Attack

This book marked a transition in the course from a primarily moral analysis of corporate responsibility to a legal and historical analysis. Yet all consistency was not lost. First, the book focuses primarily not on the use of civil but on the criminal law, which is infused with greater moral content in both theory and practice. Second, *Corporate Crime Under Attack* continued the emphasis on *story*. Its centerpiece is a look at the corporate decisions which led to Ford Motor Company's marketing its unsafe Pinto automobile, the deaths of three Indiana girls who were driving one, and the subsequent prosecution of Ford Motor Company for reckless homicide. Finally, the Pinto case provided a classic scenario by which to apply concepts of corporate collective responsibility that were introduced in the previous text.

The first half of the book provides a broad social, legal, and historical context for the detailed discussion of the Pinto case, which comprises the final half. One purpose of the early chapters is to lay the foundation for a deeper understanding of today's uneasy alliance between corporations, which are collective entities, and the criminal law, which emphasizes individual culpability. Historically, the implications of this incongruency for the moral and legal accountability of business corporations have been enormous. Another purpose is to demonstrate in dramatic terms just how costly corporate and white collar crimes are to society--not only economically, but socially and physically as well. A third purpose of the introductory chapters is to justify the authors' cautious optimism that the law is beginning to respond to a general social movement against white collar crime that began in the post-Watergate era. While the reading level of these chapters is rather rigorous, on the basis of their quizzes and papers most students comprehended the material reasonably well.

The story of the Pinto case in the final chapters was very well received by students, who welcomed the return to story after spending some time in the theoretical wilderness. Many of the principles pertaining to collective and individual moral responsibility introduced in the French book applied to the Pinto case. It was clear that the philosophical foundation laid earlier in the course led to richer class discussions, with less emphasis on individual personalities and legal technicalities. Toward the end of our Pinto discussions I assigned the Johnson & Johnson Tylenol case, where the company acted quickly and responsibly to incidents of product tampering over which they had no direct control. The positive way that company's management handled its crisis provided a dynamic contrast to Ford's inept handling of its unsafe product.

Our final class discussions focused on two disparate issues. The first concerned important developments in the sentencing of convicted white collar criminals. We studied the new guidelines established by the U.S. Sentencing Commission, which recently revised the way federal judges must approach the punishment of corporations and their executives. The final topic for the semester concerned what, if any, impact the insider trading scandals of the 1980s--and the criminal prosecutions which followed--have had on Wall Street behavior.

The students conducted three phone interviews during their reading of *Corporate Crime Under Attack*. The first was with the prosecutor who tried the Ford Pinto case. Students were fascinated with his explanation of how a conservative, law-and-order Republican could have gotten involved in what some have labeled a liberal, anti-business prosecution. The core of his answer was that certain irresponsible ways of doing business were criminal, and for him crime transcends ideology. (Student evaluations would later indicate that a majority felt that this was the most memorable interview of the semester.)

The second and third interviewees addressed the recent sentencing developments and insider trading on Wall Street, respectively. A federal district court judge appointed by President Reagan to the bench in 1984 discussed quite candidly his opposition to the U.S. Sentencing Commission's new guidelines, and explained his approach to sentencing both white collar and street criminals. The final interview was with a successful Wall Street executive and WIU alumnus who has worked in the securities field for nearly two decades. The crimes of Ivan Boesky and Michael Milken were merely symptomatic of the restructuring of institutions and values on Wall Street during the 1980s. He explained how the massive concentration of investment power in the hands of fewer firms, along with increasing pressure for short term returns, made such crimes almost inevitable. He also discussed the interesting concept of community values on Wall Street, which was something that disappeared as more and more number-crunching MBA graduates took control of investment strategies. The semester's final interview came to an appropriate end when a student noted the paradox of how the fast-track, Wall Street executive appeared to be exposing his traditional Midwestern community roots and values. The interviewee paused, then quietly answered that he often hoped and prayed that he could continue to do so.

IN RETROSPECT: DID IT WORK?

Most indications are that the course was a success. My student evaluations were among the highest I have received in fifteen years of teaching, averaging 4.39 on a 5 point scale. (This despite the one student, out of twenty, who marked the lowest possible rating for every single survey item concerning both course content and pedagogy!) In addition, the extensive written evaluations submitted by students revealed that many of the instructional techniques developed or adopted for this course--especially the speakerphone interviews, "seven-step" case analysis, individual writing assignments, and fiction readings-- were perceived by students to have contributed to an interesting, effective, and memorable course. The evaluations also confirmed my suspicions that some other aspects of the course, such as the group projects, were less successful. Yet, given that I was both exploring new territory and teaching the course for the first time, I was generally pleased that student response was so positive.

More personally, however, I have a nagging feeling that many opportunities to meaningfully affect the heads and hearts of my students--as good teaching of ethics and moral philosophy can--had been lost over the course of the semester. This is due at least in part to my attempt to cover too much ground. Had my interdisciplinary ambitiousness bested my ability to keep students focused on fundamental moral and legal principles? In trying to keep the course content "interesting" from beginning to end, did I unwittingly choose breadth over depth of study or, worse yet, prize entertainment over educational values? Or are my expectations for a single undergraduate course on business ethics simply unrealistic? In any event, I cannot say with any confidence that students who entered the course holding extremely relativistic or absolutist moral stances were significantly affected one way or the other.

Yet my outlook for this course is not a despairing one. I learned much from developing and teaching this course, and will learn even more as I revise and offer it in coming semesters. In addition to spending more time on fundamental principles and less on ephemeral issues, I will also increase the role of literature in future offerings of this course. Why? Because I have found that a well-chosen short story will more successfully *engage students at more and deeper levels* than will the typical case study in law or business. Whereas such case studies too often present a one-dimensional conflict between purely rational, economically motivated persons, literature presents the thought, motivation and action of moral agents in all of their glorious complexity, including the baser as well as nobler instincts. If the interdisciplinary vision I have for this course is ever to be realized, it will be literature that takes me all the way there.

IMPLEMENTING ETHICS ACROSS THE CURRICULUM

Mary Navarre
Department of Education
Aquinas College

The implementation of ethics as a component of all courses across the curriculum is a work in progress at Aquinas College. Although it would seem a natural and integral part of the curriculum of a college with a long and strong tradition of Catholic Christian teaching, such is not the case.

I offer these reflections on our current process because I think they might be similar for many colleges wanting to make an effort toward the inclusion of ethics and moral reflection in their curriculum, regardless of the presence or absence of a religious tradition.

Setting of Aquinas College

Aquinas is a liberal arts college in southwestern Michigan. A visitor to the campus is immediately impressed with its sylvan beauty and serene atmosphere. In the words of one such recent visitor, Aquinas is like Shakespeare's "green world," that is, a wooded area where students have the space, tranquility and liberty to examine their beliefs, discover their strengths and return, eventually, to the "real" world prepared to make it a better place. Aquinas enrolls approximately 3,000 full and part-time students. Founded by the Grand Rapids Dominican Sisters as a teacher education college for its members, it expanded its doors in 1931, to become the first coeducational Catholic college in the country.

Opening the cover of the Aquinas College catalog, the reader is faced with two pages, two messages, two facing and possibly conflicting statements. On the left hand page, the mission statement, succinct and similar to most other mission statements, reads: *The mission of Aquinas College is to provide a liberal arts education with a career orientation in a Catholic Christian context to all students capable* of profiting from such an education regardless of their gender, age, religion, ethnicity, racial background, or disability." On the right hand page a statement of diversity promises a commitment to equality, the blessings of diversity and a promise of respect and sensitivity as well as a resolve to diversify all levels of participation from Board of Trustees to faculty, students and staff. This increasing commitment to diversity comes with a price that is not at first apparent.

First impressions are of a place that is warm, friendly, open and comfortable; some would say the "niceness" is as pervasive as the creeping "kudzu" that invades our woods each Spring. Yet any mention of overtly teaching ethics or values as part of the curriculum is met with skepticism, caution and occasionally overt hostility. For Aquinas College, like many of its counterparts, is a long way from the Catholic "ghetto" of the 60's. The price of adapting to contemporary times, however, has been a mixed blessing. Aquinas is not alone in its struggle to reconcile the differences between the commitment to diversify and its identity as a Catholic college, as well as its tradition as an educational institution committed to the values espoused by both the founding sisters of the college and the country in general.

The danger of Catholic colleges losing their special identity has recently been addressed by the ACCU, Association of Catholic Colleges and Universities. This loss of identity is believed to be due to several factors: basic demographic shifts, declining numbers of religious available to teach and administer and staff the schools, faculties and student bodies who are no longer mostly Catholic, and Catholic students who enter with a deficient knowledge of and experience in their own spirituality and faith life.[1]

While the Catholic college is more ecumenical and more diverse than ever before, it is also less sure of its unique identity as a Catholic college. Given this diversity in administration and students, the challenge is how to connect students with their faith and its rich intellectual tradition, and how to go about informing students with the habits of ethical reflection and behavior. While these philosophical considerations may be built into some disciplines, such as literature, philosophy, religious studies, this is often an additional challenge for the natural and social sciences as well as for the professional schools.

According to Kenneth Woodward, "In the struggle to survive at any cost, many marginal schools have become marginally Catholic."[2] Some would say this is true of Aquinas College. Woodward's challenge is particularly acute when applied to the area of ethics. No one suggests that a teacher or a curriculum is "value-free," for that in itself *is* a value. Nevertheless, one is left with the question of what Aquinas students do learn about ethics and moral reflection from their professors.

Aquinas people have always had, in the words of one long tenured professor, "parallel" values. There are no serial killers here; most are fine upstanding citizens. There are differing opinions on the inflammatory topics of abortion, birth control, sex and AIDS, but we often choose not to face the issues or the differences among us. Many feel such discussions can lead to no good. Failure to agree, some say, will only cause hard feelings and dissent. As a result, the issue of ethics and moral reflection has been left to the philosophers and the religious studies professors. The rest may dabble in moral issues briefly, but cautiously if at all. While it may seem not only feasible, but essential for a Catholic college to concern itself with ethics across the curriculum, it is a topic many persons would rather leave alone.

The Obstacles

There are several specific forces working against the integration of ethics across the curriculum. I have categorized these obstacles under the headings of paranoia, pitfalls and paralysis.

Paranoia

There is an irony in the fact that Aquinas College, a college rooted in the Catholic Christian tradition, has unique obstacles to the effort. While all colleges are addressing the problem of ethics, Aquinas and other religious institutions have some unique obstacles inherent because of its personnel. Many faculty members feel inadequate and threatened by the thought of directly teaching Catholic ethics or any other ethics, since this is outside their area of expertise. Others feel uncomfortable that non-Catholics might attempt to represent the teachings of the Church on issues of ethics and moral reflection. Questions arise: What ethics ought to be taught? Who should teach it? Who should take the classes? Ought these be required?

Originally staffed largely by Grand Rapids Dominican sisters, their numbers now constitute only about 15-20% of the total number of faculty and staff. Although between 75-80% of our incoming freshmen declare themselves Catholic, there are no statistics available on the number of faculty and staff who do, since this question is not asked of them. Some members identify themselves as Catholics formed by the pre-Vatican II church, others are disillusioned institutional Catholics, formed by the Church in their youth but staying away from it as adults. Some refer to themselves as "closet" Catholics, quiet and almost apologetic for their alliance with Catholicism. There are non-Catholics from various Christian traditions, persons from the Jewish tradition, and others who claim no religious formation but espouse the general Judeo-Christian values of society. There are no priests or members of men's religious orders presently on the faculty. This diversity among faculty, then, adds to an atmosphere of caution and insecurity around the topic of ethics.

Pitfalls

Indoctrination is an especially sensitive topic for those steeped in the Dominican tradition. While advocating the vigorous exchange of intellectual ideas, the history of Dominicans includes the ignominious events of the infamous "Spanish inquisition." The freedom of the individual's moral conscience must be zealously guarded in every age, no less in this age of diversity and recognition of a pluralistic society. Propaganda and coercion have no place in any university or college--Catholic or otherwise.

As an antidote to indoctrination, values clarification emerged in the late 60's and early 70's. This ill-fated movement is recent enough to be remembered by members of the current faculty. Its dissolution into relativism is also remembered. Both are recalled as a "cautionary tale" of what can happen when incompetents dabble in the lofty world of ethics.

Yet another antidote to indoctrination is that of "developmentalism." The research of Kohlberg, Dewey and Piaget led to the notion that moral judgements are best developed through the students' own efforts to grapple with moral dilemmas with their *peers* and without teacher intervention.

In either case, as is succinctly written by a current faculty member at Aquinas, "The dilemma, then, is this. On the one hand, the moral educator is urged to refrain from indoctrinating students. On the other hand, this same educator, through conviction and commitment, must motivate students to become ever more willing to engage in moral reflection and decision-making, whether this means gaining new insights into their own value systems or confronting those values as possibly inadequate."[3]

Another pitfall is lack of ownership for the curriculum and turf wars. Although the curriculum is the primary work and responsibility of the faculty, the years have resulted in many individual faculty members protecting their "pet" courses and requirements. Still another pitfall to the implementation of ethics is in the very method by which decisions are made about courses and curriculum. Committees work on the original designs and then bring their ideas before the entire membership at monthly Academic Assembly meetings. These formal settings offer a public forum for those who flourish in this arena. Yet the same forum intimidates and silences others who do not function best in this environment. Political savvy, rather than the best interest of the college and its students, can result in decisions that are detrimental to the implementation of programs addressing topics such as ethics and moral reflection across the curriculum.

Paralysis

There is often a tendency in human nature to maintain the "status quo." This is particularly true in situations where many members have passed or are presently engaged in mid-life transitions and are looking forward to retirement. This is the case with many faculty and staff at Aquinas. Some will try to stop any effort to change the curriculum to include ethics because of fear of losing their jobs. Others are alienated from the college community, and still others are resistant to change simply because they have already seen too much change in their lifetimes. Continual retrenchment, low salaries and downsizing of faculty and staff have contributed to low morale and apathy.

For all of these reasons, then, there is a tendency to do nothing about changing the curriculum or including ethics as part of the curriculum.

The Helps

Inclusion

A rare opportunity presents itself this academic year. Believing that "...general education is primarily the work of the faculty, their role in its reshaping should be primary, and since general education is the chief work of the college, the administration should identify its reshaping as a priority over the next few years,"[4] a task force was formed to study and offer suggestions for the revision of the general education requirements.

Prior to the 1970's, Aquinas curriculum requirements included twelve hours of theology, many other specific requirements and very few options. The "new" curriculum was essentially a cafeteria plan. There were few requirements; students merely selected courses from six categories: natural sciences, social sciences, aesthetics, perspectives, personal development and a "catchall category" of language, communication and mathematics. Over the past 20 plus years, a proliferation of classes has resulted, as well as a fragmentation of the goal of providing students with a liberal arts education. Students may graduate with a "pastiche" of credits rather than a coherent body of knowledge and skills.

In October, 1992, the Aquinas Board of Trustees mandated a plan which included a two year study on general education. The appointment of the task force and the commencement of the study provide Aquinas the opportunity to "walk the walk" and not just "talk the talk" of ethical decision making and moral reflection in the general education requirements. Determined to include the thoughts and ideas of the entire college community, the committee established multiple opportunities for faculty and staff to meet and discuss the profile of the Aquinas student. In open forums the importance of moral reflection and ethics as an integral part of the curriculum was discussed. Although not viewed as an overwhelming concern of the participants, ethics and morality were mentioned in most groups as one of the most important goals of the educated person.

Following the open forum discussions on the profile of the Aquinas graduate, several focus groups have been formed to study and make recommendations to the task force for curriculum revision. Topics include critical thinking, gender issues, writing, global and multi-cultural awareness, and American pluralism. Another is on ethics. Although it is too early to predict the recommendations of this committee, their readings and study of the topic will be an essential part of the information used to reform the curriculum. Moral reflection inevitably occurs in most of the focus groups. For example, one cannot discuss issues of gender or pluralism and diversity without touching on the essence of justice and human worth. Service learning, with its emphasis on service to the poor and disenfranchised, addresses the inequality of the distribution of wealth and opportunity. Consequently, there is a high probability that their recommendations will result in the inclusion of moral reflection as an integral part of the curriculum. The fact that the entire Aquinas community of faculty, staff and students is included in the focus groups will assure a sense of ownership for the eventual product by most of the community.

Inspiration

Several unforeseen and unexpected moments have occurred that may provide continual inspiration for the work ahead. One was the formation of a task force on ethics and Catholic teaching which was called together during the academic year 1992-3. The work of that task force came to completion in the Spring of 1993 when the entire college community accepted a Statement on Ethics and Catholic Teaching, a copy of which is appended. As one can see, the college seeks to protect both the Catholic intellectual tradition with its concern for faith and academic freedom's valuing of the "vigorous exchange of ideas."

A recurring metaphor for the Aquinas tradition is that of guests invited to the banquet of moral discourse and truth seeking. As stated in the document: "Aquinas College...firmly rooted in the Catholic intellectual tradition, invites all to the table of moral discourse."[5] Rather than an atmosphere of coercion or proselytizing, the context is one of welcome to a space where ideas can be exchanged and change can take place as persons engage in the search for truth in the context of a tolerant and respectful community.

Much to the surprise of the task force members, the document was accepted unanimously and with little argument. There was only a hesitance grounded in the practical question of how to provide this atmosphere in order to aid our students to become the ethical decision makers we value. A second phenomenon is a renewed interest in the study of the college's heritage, specifically the life and times of St. Thomas Aquinas and St. Dominic as well as the beliefs that inspired their lives. This study and interest supported by programs through Campus Ministry lead us to reflection on Aristotle's philosophy and a promotion of Aristotle's virtue ethics as a forerunner of the college's Thomistic heritage.

A fortifying corollary to the study of Thomistic philosophy is the effect of this writer's two summers at Marquette University's Center for the Study of Ethics. The weeks of study served to renew and revitalize a commitment to ethics across the curriculum which, in turn, has been infused into focus groups, task forces and committee meetings.

Yet another route for the infusion of ethics has been in the Freshman Humanities Experience. Through this program, required of all incoming freshmen, Catholics and non-Catholics alike are afforded the opportunity to study and discuss ethics and moral reflection in the context of the Aristotelian tradition. In all of these ways then, faculty, staff and students have had the opportunity to receive inspiration to incorporate and benefit from the infusion of ethical reflection in both the curriculum and in co-curricular activities.

Integration

Not only in the curriculum, but also in life outside of the curriculum of study, ethics and moral reflection need to be integrated. Coherence, comprehensiveness and issues of commonality need to be concentrated in the general education curriculum, and moral reflection needs to be included in the content of many courses. However, it is not enough to end the effort there. Living out the tradition of the moral life needs to extend beyond the curriculum. Aquinas College is committed to graduating alumni who will continue to make positive contributions to society through their own ethical living. To this end, extracurricular activities in the way of service learning, volunteer work, and student services will flow from the general education plan. Faculty and staff need to collaborate with each other to reinforce the benefits of an integrated cohesive program of study, work and life.

Further efforts to improve offerings on the issue of ethics will be experienced through forums on great issues, newsletters, guest speakers, and faculty sharing their own experiences with each other. The precedent for this already exists in TQM (Total Quality Management) meetings which occur regularly for faculty to come together and discuss what works for them along such mundane lines as developing syllabi, planning courses, evaluating student papers and evoking student discussions.

Conclusions

The work is in progress; the jury is still out. In three years a new core curriculum will be in place with a major emphasis on ethics across the curriculum. The world will be only a few years away from the turn of the millennium--only one more turn in the universe of stars, like every other--but in the place where humans dwell and human imagination takes flight it will be perhaps a time for extraordinary energy to make this planet a better dwelling place for all of its inhabitants. Aquinas College plans to be a part of this world, graduating students who are grounded in the ethical tradition of this college and capable of the moral reflection and decision making needed in these most complex of times.

Notes

1. "Strategic Plan Implementation Program," Association of Catholic Colleges and Universities, 1 Dupont Circle, Suite 650, Washington D.C. 20036. Unpublished.

2. Woodward, Kenneth. "Catholic Higher Education: What Happened?" *Commonweal.* April 9, 1993, p. 13-18.

3. Williams, Michael. "The Dilemma of Moral Education: Indifference or Indoctrination?" *The Living Light* 15:3, 1978, p. 399-405.

4. Blomme, Michael, et. al. "General Education Project submitted to Lily Endowment Workshop for the Liberal Arts, The Colorado College at Colorado Springs," June 25, 1993. Aquinas College, Grand Rapids, MI. Unpublished.

5. Marko, Robert. "Working Paper of Foundational Statement." Spring, 1993, Aquinas College, Grand Rapids, MI. Unpublished.

Appendix

WORKING PAPER OF FOUNDATIONAL STATEMENT

The mission of Aquinas College is to provide a liberal arts education with a career orientation in a Catholic Christian context to all students capable of profiting from such an education regardless of their sex, age, religion, ethnicity, or racial background.

The Task Force on Ethics and Catholic Teaching has been mandated to more fully articulate the identity of Aquinas College and to explore the place within the college of the Judeo-Christian ethical tradition and religious teaching, with full respect to other religious traditions, academic freedom, and personal conscience.

In this context, *Catholic* refers to an identity that is open. As Sr. Marie Celeste Miller, O.P., expressed in the beginning of this strategic planning process:

The Catholic perspective on ethical matters and social teachings of the Church are taught in an environment which allows the discussion of other perspectives and the preservation of an ecumenical stance toward other religions and orientations. The Catholic and Dominican tradition of this college has always been inclusive rather than exclusive, not narrow and alienating.[1]

Therefore, while recognizing the Catholic Christian tradition of Aquinas, we readily acknowledge the differences and diversity that exist here. While Aquinas College is not simply a "marketplace of ideas," given the Catholic tradition of Aquinas and its traditional concern for

---

[1] Sr. Marie Celeste expressed this as a clarification of objective 1.1 of Goal 1 of Strategic Plan - 1992. The goal was approved by the Board of Trustees on October 20, 1992.

faith, moral character and virtue, challenging ideas have always been welcome here.[2] Academic freedom has always functioned on the operational level of this institution. The right and responsibility of academic freedom, as spelled out in the faculty handbook, is fully protected.[3] The vigorous exchange of ideas is at the very core of intellectual life; Aquinas welcomes that exchange.

The Catholic tradition here at Aquinas is non-proselytizing. As *Dignitatis Humanae* (Vatican II's Decree on Religious Freedom) affirms, all are immune to coercion especially in matters of religious belief.[4] Our human dignity calls us to seek the truth and live it out. Aquinas College supports individuals in this personal journey. Christian theology, in fact, holds that religious faith is by its nature free and thus Aquinas does not impose nor coerce members of the college community in matters religious.

---

[2] James Heft argues why a Catholic institution is not simply a marketplace of ideas in his essay, "Academic Freedom and the Catholic Community" in *Theology and the University*. John Apczynski, ed. New York: University of America, 1987, pp. 207-236. The committee is indebted to Sr. Mary James Rau, O.P. for materials on the history of the college and its mission. See also Mona Schwind, O.P., *Period Pieces: An Account of the Grand Rapids Dominican, 1853-1966*. Grand Rapids: Sisters of St. Dominic, 1991, for the founding of the college, particularly chapters 11 and 15.

[3] Academic freedom is dealt with in Section H-6 of the faculty handbook. In addition to Heft cited above, see Avery Dulles, "The Teaching Mission of the Church and Academic Freedom," *America*. Vol. 162. April 21, 1990, pp. 397-402.

[4] See *Dignitatis Humanae*, particularly paragraphs 3 and 4. Mary Lea Schneider, O.S.F., argues that American pragmatism also guarantees this freedom of learning and freedom of research. See her "The Social Ecology of the American Catholic College," *Horizons*. Vol. 18. Spring, 1991, pp. 63-73.

This Catholic Christian identity of Aquinas embraces what Bishop James Malone identified as three characteristics that ought to be present in Catholic universities and colleges: 1) sacramental awareness; 2) a sense of community; and 3) a pursuit of real truth.[5] First, a sacramental awareness affirms that all life is permeated with the holy. One encounters a God who is present and mediated in human history, events and lives. The college provides opportunities for sacramental celebration and spiritual growth for those who wish to avail themselves of them. Second, a person's growth in faith is supported and experienced in community. A sense of community encourages our seeking together the common good, a project which paradoxically fulfills us as individuals.

Lastly, Aquinas, a college in the Dominican tradition, is committed to the search for truth, *Veritas*. Thomas Aquinas encountered truth and the good wherever it could be found; for him that search entailed the pagan philosophy of Aristotle. In academic language, Athens does have something to say to Jerusalem. Nonetheless, this search for truth is not simply conducted in the post-Enlightenment rationalistic manner, but is a journey open to mystery, acknowledging human limitations.

The college's experience of and reputation for hospitality where individual persons are seen and received as guests make possible this common search for truth grounded in a sacramental awareness. Henri Nouwen probably best describes this characteristic of hospitality that Aquinas exemplifies so well:

> Hospitality, therefore, means primarily the creation of
> a free space where the stranger can enter and become
> a friend instead of an enemy. Hospitality is not to
> change people, but to offer them space where change

---

[5] Malone makes this claim in a June 26, 1992 address on Catholic higher education. For the text, see James Malone, "A University's Catholic Identity: Assertive, But Not Sectarian," *Origins*. Vol. 22. July 23, 1991, pp. 166-168.

can take place. It is not to bring men and women over to our side, but to offer freedom not disturbed by dividing lines. It is not to lead our neighbor into a corner where there are not alternatives left, but to open a wide spectrum of options for choice and commitment. It is not an educated intimidation with good books, good stories and good works, but the liberation of fearful hearts so that words can find roots and bear ample fruit. It is not a method of making our God and our way into the criteria of happiness but the opening of an opportunity to others to find their God and their way.[6]

Hospitality, therefore, means much more than simply being nice; hospitality is a creation of space where students, teachers and staff learn and grow in a mutually respectful and challenging atmosphere.

It is within the above context that Aquinas faculty and staff are encouraged to address questions of faith and meaning, values and ethics. As a Catholic Christian liberal arts college with a career orientation, we pride ourselves on being an institution that commits itself to fostering a sense of ethics in our students for a career as well as for life. We want our students to become ethical decision makers and to use their gifts and talents in service of others.[7]

---

[6] Henri Nouwen, *Reaching Out: The Three Movements of the Spiritual Life.* Garden City, NJ: Doubleday, 1975, p. 51. Nouwen's notion of hospitality is a central theme in Parker J. Palmer, *To Know as We Are Known: A Spirituality of Education.* San Francisco: Harper & Row, 1983.

[7] This has been a theme of President Paul Nelson's vision of the college. See Richard N. Bolles, *How to Find Your Mission in Life.* (Berkeley: Ten Speed Press, 1991) for an articulation of how one's mission is an intersection of the work that one most needs to do and the world most needs to be done.

We recognize that we are living in a time of tremendous change. Some scholars claim that the moral umbrella of the Judeo-Christian tradition has collapsed; others argue that in light of cultural diversity moral discourse itself is not possible. Aquinas College, on the other hand, firmly rooted in the Judeo-Christian ethical tradition, invites all to the table of moral discourse. As we discern truth, we acknowledge our individual biases, we seek our common ground, and we ask that all be tolerant of the views and beliefs of others. As a beginning step, the committee suggests that open forums, discussions, lectures and debates may continue to keep the conversation alive and Aquinas College a community of moral discourse.

BEAUTY VS. AESTHETICS:
ETHICS IN THE FINE ARTS CURRICULUM

Arthur Pontynen
Department of Art
University of Wisconsin - Oshkosh

It is a commonplace assumption today that ethics should not be taught within the typical college fine arts curriculum. There are those who claim that art and ethics are separate realms. There are those who claim that since ethics is ultimately subjective, then including ethics within the fine arts is distracting at best, oppressive at worst. The distraction lies in the assumption that ethics is merely a matter of personal opinion; the oppression lies in the assumption that presenting an ethical vision within the context of a fine arts curriculum can only be done by arbitrarily and aggressively promoting one willful preference to the exclusion of others. But there is something disingenuous about these claims.

The question is not *whether* ethics should be taught; the teaching of ethics is right now at the very heart of the typical fine arts curriculum. Nor need we be limited to the question: *"Whose* ethics should we teach, or rather impose upon, the viewer?" There is a third possibility, commonly neglected today--rather than whether, or whose, ethics will be taught, we might better consider: *"What* ethical visions can be taught?"

These three options refer to three primary and contending cultural traditions vying for our allegiance today. Those traditions are: art for art's sake, art for politics' sake, and art in the pursuit of wisdom. These three traditions perennially result in distinct visions not only of art, but of science and ethics as well. They result also in advocating distinct cultural goals. Art for art's sake, and art for politics' sake, focus on the pursuit of aesthetics. Art dedicated to wisdom focuses on the pursuit of beauty. To the point, these three cultural perspectives cannot simultaneously be pursued without succumbing to an incoherent and debilitating confusion. A choice must be made.

This is evidenced by the fact that today art dedicated to the pursuit of wisdom--of that which is true, good, and consequently beautiful--is commonly neglected. For what? Either art that is produced for its own sake, or art that is produced for political purposes, that is, for the sake of power. It is the clear conflict between art produced for its own sake (Modernism), and art that is political (Postmodernism), that marks much of the turmoil in our culture today.

Consequently, two conflicting cultural visions today enjoy center stage--Modernism and Postmodernism. The terms Modernism and Postmodernism here refer to a particular set of beliefs (explained below) rather than mere chronological or sociological categories. In contrast are those numerous and distinct traditions commonly dedicated to pursuing wisdom (e.g. Classicism, Confucianism, Victorianism, Christianity, Judaism, Islam, Buddhism, Hinduism, etc.). In education today, those traditions committed to the pursuit of wisdom are rarely granted a podium. The Modernists and Postmodernists claim: leave moralizing to the pundits, the metaphysicians and the propagandists; our concern is with getting the facts right, and with personal creativity and style.

BEAUTY VS AESTHETICS

It is those traditions dedicated to the pursuit of wisdom that are concerned with beauty. Those traditions hold that beauty is associated with understanding, with becoming cognizant of, the ultimate purpose of life--be it viewed in terms of teleology, cosmology, or both. As a cognitive activity, beauty is linked with an understanding of that which is true and good in reality, not as a matter of taste or opinion, but to some precious degree as a matter of knowledge. Beauty, then, is the embodiment and splendor of wisdom. Whereas wisdom seeking art properly focuses on the pursuit of beauty, both Modernism and Post-modernism focus on aesthetic taste.

Rather than being concerned with obtaining glimpses of wisdom, aesthetics aims at presenting a coherent personal statement. Given a set of assumptions, or a socially preferred set of facts, then one's style in art or life ought to effectively express those assumptions. That is, aesthetic taste is a non-cognitive activity. A focus on aesthetic taste takes for granted that art does not explain life or reality, but rather it expresses an ultimately subjective yet coherent vision of life and the world.

Whether we are involved in art, science, the humanities, or commerce, by examining the three general traditions that inform our activities--art (science, culture, money) for its' own sake, for the sake of politics, or for the pursuit of wisdom--it will be shown that at the core of these traditions lie three distinct ethical visions. So distinct that they cannot simultaneously be adopted and valued.

The dilemma then is not *whether* we should consider ethics to be a part of our educational goals; for better or worse ethics already is taught. And perhaps we are not limited to *whose* ethics shall we impose. Perhaps the real question is *what* types of ethics can we celebrate? Perhaps the real issue is how might we transcend the Modernist and Postmodernist notions of aesthetic taste by aspiring to the realm of beauty.

ART FOR ART'S SAKE: A CRITIQUE OF THE MODERNIST PARADIGM

Is it not a commonplace assumption that the task of education is to provide a wide variety of accurate facts to students so that upon graduation those students will be able to build a lifestyle, an aesthetic of existence, grounded upon a factual basis? The scholar is to make certain that the facts presented are accurate, and the student is to enjoy the pleasure of selecting from the facts those which are attractive in building a world-view, a lifestyle. Facts are put then into aesthetic structures that are the personal products of each individual student's imagination.

This assumption underlying the typical college curriculum is Modernist. It assumes that the student *ought* to be exposed to a wide range of descriptive facts which are as accurate and objective as possible. The student is to accumulate those facts for four years, and at least upon graduation the student *ought* to construct a personal narrative, a personal vision, of life. The assumption then is that this process is impartial, tolerant, and untainted by dogmatism or ideological cant. It assumes that the collection and transmission of facts, to be used in the personal development of a lifestyle that is fact based and coherent is the key to a culture both pluralistic and free. *Aesthetic taste is deemed normative.*

In concordance, art history courses are commonly concerned with two essential tasks. The first is to establish what are the facts of the case, and the second task is to construct a chronological and explanatory account of the history of art objects.

It is assumed that each work of art has a place within a historical narrative, and efforts are made to discuss what those works of art meant within that historical narrative. In addition, it is assumed that each work of art has intrinsic stylistic qualities that make it a unique aesthetic experience, and those stylistic qualities are to be analyzed and appreciated.

Similarly, studio art classes are commonly concerned with making current what art history treats nostalgically. That entails cultivating an expressive creativity via the development of a personal style of art. A central concern of studio art is in helping individuals express themselves aesthetically.

Creativity is understood as referring to the imagination, and it is assumed that the imaginative faculty is something that cannot be taught, but can be nurtured. It is further assumed that the content of the products of the imaginative faculty cannot be qualitatively judged, but the effectiveness of their formal expression can be. Works of art, then, combine discernible technical skill with a personal vision.

That combination of subjectivism with coherency of realization, of presentation, constitutes aesthetic taste. In nurturing our ability to express our personal vision of life we cultivate good taste. It is good taste that reflects the skillful combination of imagination with style. It is the combination of imagination with style that constitutes Modernist culture.

This paradigm presents two initial problems facing those teaching in the humanities and the fine arts; the first is whether people really need training in constructing consistent, coherent, or rather, aesthetic lifestyles. The second problem is whose selection of facts shall we present and in what type of historical narrative should we place those facts?

Is it really so difficult to learn to be aesthetic, to develop a consistent vision of life free from contradiction? Is it so difficult to recognize that, given a set of assumptions, then certain necessary conclusions result, and that, should one change those assumptions, then the conclusions change as well? Is a coherent creativity really worthy of constituting an academic major in the college curriculum, much less the goal of education? Or can it easily be substituted by the general reminders that, in our daily activities, assumptions affect conclusions and contradictions commonly make no sense?

Similar questions can be raised concerning the selection and collection of facts. It is typical that in the humanities, in art history, and even in science, certain objects are assumed to be works of art, assumed to be significant, and then a descriptive and nostalgic narrative text is written about those objects. The art historian decides or accepts which objects are important, and then typically attempts to discern what those objects, those works of art, meant--not what they mean. Excluded is the propriety of seeking from works of art vital insight, perennial wisdom, dare we say Truth, concerning the human condition or more.

Likewise, the studio artist accepts or decides that certain objects, or rather, concerns, are significant, and then attempts to express those concerns aesthetically. The produced work of art should effectively express its content, should be formally consistent, coherent, and expressive of the personal imagination of the artist.

But if both art history and studio consist of accumulation of arbitrarily selected objects, if both the selection of facts and the production of objects deemed art are nostalgic, arbitrary, and subjective processes, then what is being taught in the way of values? Given that aesthetic taste is subjective and personal, then the arts might well be a lofty form of entertainment, or a not so lofty nexus for sensitivity training, worthy perhaps of our personal interest, but not that of our educational institutions. Why? Because *de gustibus non disputandum*-- there is no disputing taste! The conclusion then is clear: there may be facts, but how we select those facts in building a cultural vision is ultimately an arbitrary (though perhaps stylish) construct. Neither art history nor studio art offer us a glimpse of wisdom or beauty.

Consequently, one is hard pressed to justify the Modernist vision of the fine arts or the humanities. To reduce art history and studio art to the study of arbitrarily selected nostalgic facts and coherent imaginative structures is to deny the intrinsic validity of culture as the object of academic discourse. Why? Because the essence of arbitrary and nostalgic selection, of aesthetic taste, is anti-intellectual. It permits little thought. It relies ultimately upon the will.

The suggestion has been made, however, that the manufacture and selection of those objects known as art stems from genius, and that the contemplation of the works of individual genius, or those resulting from the collective genius of groups of people, will indeed inspire us and make us more sensitive of other visions of life.

But in the name of such sensitivity and tolerance, who is treated insensitively and intolerantly? Anyone who is suspicious of claims of genius and anyone who believes that glimpses of wisdom and beauty are obtainable. That is, virtually all of the cultures around the world for thousands of years that are neither Modernist nor Postmodernist.

Pleas for sensitivity, for aesthetic taste, for the primacy of feelings devoid of truth, require that all traditions that believe in wisdom and beauty are really merely aesthetic taste masquerading as "beauty," that assertions of wisdom and beauty are hypocritical at best, deceptive at worst. It requires that all of the art of millennia be reduced to the realm of opinion and lifestyle. It requires that we view the past and even the present as arbitrary narratives that imprison us. Aesthetic taste espouses freedom and tolerance, but tragically reduces culture to the triumph of the will.

THE ETHICS OF MODERNIST ART AND SCIENCE

It is a mistaken assumption that ethics is not in fact being taught in art history and studio classes, much less in all the other disciplines that constitute the Modernist academic curriculum. It is assumed by many that ethics is not and ought not be part of the process of accumulating historical facts or nurturing the creative imagination. It is all too commonly, and falsely, assumed that the accumulation of facts and the cultivation of the creative imagination are objective activities devoid of ethical content, that in science, the humanities, or the fine arts, ethics and aesthetics do not mix. But they do.

Modernism argues for the cultivation of a coherent personal vision of life. The student is to accumulate facts, and construct a coherent lifestyle, just as the artist or the citizen is to do the same. What, then, is the ethical content of much of contemporary education, although the very mention of ethics being an intrinsic part of all disciplines is viewed by many as inappropriate?

Addressing this question requires a bit of background concerning the foundations of Modernism. Part of the Enlightenment, Modernism takes for granted that reason and empirical facts will free us from superstition and ignorance. Medieval debates concerning how human freedom and dignity can coexist with truth and with an omnipotent and omniscient God, shifted during the Enlightenment to a debate concerning how human freedom and dignity can coexist with facts, with descriptive and predictive data. This question is the central justification for the fine arts and the humanities in a scientific milieu.

The perennial problem of how *obedience to truth* can set us free took on a new slant: how can *obedience to facts* set us free? In a world of predictive and descriptive facts, can humanity be viewed other than as a machine or the product of nature or nurture? Free from any notions of truth, of ultimate purpose, are we then liberated, or newly condemned to embrace a purposeless teleology or cosmology? In either case, do human dignity and freedom make sense, or are they but endearing illusions?

It is the Modernist strain of the Enlightenment that stated clearly and confidently that human freedom and dignity are realizable in a world of descriptive and predictive facts.

How this is achieved is explained in the works of Immanuel Kant (1724-1804). As a primary expositor of Modernism, Kant relies on a genius-based formalism as the key to a liberating aesthetic vision. He suggests that there are descriptive facts on the one hand, and formal, indeed aesthetic, structures on the other hand. There are facts, like bricks, and how one builds a House of Life with those bricks is a matter of personal taste. Personal taste, or rather, aesthetics, offers the possibility of a wide variety of fact-based narratives that are pluralistic, coherent, and free products of the imagination. By aesthetic taste Modernists mean that art is non-cognitive (it does not attempt to explain the world), self-referential (is concerned with the intrinsic qualities of any activity), and a perfection of a kind.

Even cursory reflection reveals an implicit code of ethics accompanying this aesthetic, a code of ethics that is taught (often unreflectively) in art departments across the nation.

We are taught that we should enjoy art just as we should enjoy a friend's company, not for how that person or object can be used, or what they might tell us. Rather, we enjoy our friends for what they are, and art for what it is. A Modernist treats art (or science) as one would treat a friend, by treating it not merely as a means to an end, but as an end unto itself. As such it is about dignity, mutual respect, and a shared commitment to toleration and freedom. The term Art for art's sake is synonymous with the term Science for Science's sake, or Ethics for Ethics' sake.

In contrast to the Medieval prescription that we may do as we please if only we love, the Modernist vision is then that *we may do as we will, as long as we do no harm to others.* Is this not the central ethical premise held dear by an extraordinary number of our students and colleagues? The implicit ethical content of Modernism includes then the following: that the arts, like people, are ends unto themselves rather than merely means to an end. That individuals should be treated in accordance with their personal dignity; to use either art or people as merely means to an end is to manipulate, and to manipulate is to brutalize. Better to embrace a pluralistic tolerance, that is, aesthetic taste.

And so, we give students the facts and teach them that they *should* develop their own style, in art and life. But there are two problems with this pedagogy and this ethical teleology. First, *lifestyles do in fact come into conflict.* For example, art for art's sake is in conflict with art for the sake of power, both of which, in turn, are in conflict with art dedicated to the pursuit of wisdom. Second, the admonition that we ought to do as we will, as long as we do no harm to others *gives us not a clue as to what is worth doing.*

THE POST MODERNIST CHALLENGE TO MODERNISM

The ethical content of these Modernist principles of aesthetic taste, and their apparent failure, surround us daily. Who teaching today has not encountered those who aspire to being non-cognitive, self-referential, and a perfection of their own kind?

It is Postmodernism that pushes these Modernist principles to their logical conclusion. What is that conclusion? It is the triumph of the will. We cannot know the world, only theories of the world. There are no universal or transcendent principles, only coherent discursive constructs. Therefore, self-realization and self-expression are the only discernible goods. Could it be that the liberating notion of aesthetic taste tragically leads to the solipsistic and nihilistic willfulness of Postmodernism?

It is the Postmodernists who attack the Modernist notion that aesthetic taste is normative, declaring it a particularly ideological and hypocritical approach to education and culture. We might note that by Postmodern is not meant contemporary; not all contemporary artists or educators are Postmodernist. What then is meant by Postmodernist? Those who assume that all assertions of knowledge are theoretical, and that self-realization and self-expression are the only discernible goods (e.g. Derrida, Foucault, etc). Given these principles, then knowledge is but a mask for power, and culture is oppressive.

Modernists hold that aesthetic taste is what permits life to be dignified and diverse even within a world of descriptive and predictive facts. It is aesthetic taste that confirms freedom and dignity in the face of a scientific world that is mechanistic and jejune. It is the Postmodernists, however, who reveal the negative possibilities of aesthetic taste--that aesthetic taste, being subjective, is but a mask for power. Given that aesthetic taste is normative, then the Postmodernists rightly ask *whose* aesthetic taste shall publicly prevail? They conclude that public assertions of knowledge, of beauty, even of aesthetics, are just that--willful and oppressive. The public square is where you do it to them before they do it to you.

Aesthetic taste is the Modernist key to opening the door to individual freedom and dignity, but that same key is seen by the Postmodernists as the one that locks them into arbitrary and coercive lifestyles. It is, then, the conflict between Modernism and its progeny--Postmodernism--that brings into question common assumptions concerning aesthetics, culture, and scholarship. It is the source of many of the conflicts that surround the academy today.

The conflict is simply this: whether one is speaking of the fine arts, the humanities, or even the sciences, the Modernist paradigm suggests that we individually select facts and construct consistent narratives of meaning. The Postmodernists observe that it is a public and political issue as to which facts are selected and whose narratives are to be taught. Consequently, the Modernist argues for free speech and genius, while the Postmodernist argues that there is no such thing as free speech, only the will.

The Postmodernists assume that culture is arbitrary and hence oppressive. But if cultures include both oppressors and victims, what happens when the victims overthrow their oppressors? They can only become what they profess to hate: oppressors. And since they become what they profess to hate, then what can they hope for but their own annihilation? It takes a remarkable act of faith to conclude that the resulting process of violence and self-annihilation constitutes progress, and that the utopian goal of Postmodernism is not a nihilistic and totalitarian endgame.

To the point, the Modernists teach an ethics, but the flaws within that system of ethics are exposed by the Postmodernists. What, then, is offered instead by the Postmodernists? They offer an incoherent insistence that all traditions are merely masks for power--except their own. Consequently, virtually all of the art produced before the advent of the Enlightenment, and much of the art around the world since then is utterly wrong in its belief that what is held to be dear is even partially true.

The result: a cultural advocacy of the triumph of the will which leads to a nihilistic anti-culture culture. The dilemma then is where do we go from here?

THE THIRD OPTION: THE ISSUE OF BEAUTY

Contemporary theory challenges the Modernist status quo. The practice of art history and studio art focusing on nostalgic facts, imagination, and style, is now suspect. And yet, Postmodernism offers us little hope for the future. It is a challenge that is directed not only at the fine arts and the humanities, but science as well. It is the challenge, and failure, of Postmodernist theory that makes the study of the relationship of ethics and art not only timely, but at the very core of the intellectual disputes that surround our disciplines and campuses today. It is that challenge and failure that justifies a reconsidering of the role of ethics in teaching studio art and art history, the humanities and the sciences.

It is easy to imagine the Postmodernist response to a poet reading "Beauty is truth; truth, beauty. That is all you need to know." Since Postmodernists assume that knowledge is but a mask for power and culture is oppressive, their response in essence is: "Beauty is power; power, beauty. There is nothing you need to know." Such a response must give pause to those dedicated to culture and education. It might also lead to considering alternatives to the Modernist/Postmodernist tradition.

Given the Postmodernist observation that aesthetic taste is a mask for power and that culture is oppressive, then what happens to Keat's poem? Beauty is replaced by power, and so too is virtue.

Is it not ironic to find that ethics, the very issue held to be suspect by many today, offers the core defense of the teaching of studio and art history? It is ethics that lies at the very core of both aesthetics and beauty. But it is only beauty that effectively distinguishes civility from barbarism.

Ethics implies meaningful choice, the ability to justifiably select one course of action over another. It is the distinction of meaningful from meaningless choice that is the core issue in the fine arts and the humanities.

This issue is at the very heart and soul of culture. It is the raison d'etre for the fine arts, humanities, and for science that rises above the level of technology. For those dedicated to human freedom and dignity, culture is more than a matter of entertainment, triviality, or utility. It focuses on our dreams, our aspirations, on that which inspires and that which ennobles. In other words, it focuses on our ethics and the justification for that ethics.

How, then, can we account for a concern for the fine arts and the humanities, especially amongst those who imagine themselves to be far too sophisticated to believe that culture is anything more than mere entertainment, or those too politically astute to believe that cultural reflection has any purpose beyond the will? By noting that without the possibility of meaningful choice, then all choice is mandated to be meaningless; irony and tyranny are deemed normative. Without culture and ethics, life is reduced to a coercive triviality where no preference can be justified, and where all appetites are equally banal. A world lacking justifiable preference is a world without beauty, justice, or love. It is a world lacking in even the most basic of pleasures--friendship. It is a world without meaning.

Given that art for art's sake and art for the sake of politics fail as cultural or ethical paradigms, how might the fine arts and ethics be taught? By a shift from the willful to the cognitive. Rather than encouraging the reduction of culture to the realm of aesthetic taste, we might better explore the realm of beauty.

Modernism advocates that facts be put into coherent form, but why not focus instead on principles rather than merely facts? Why not advocate the study of virtue as the focal point of the fine arts curriculum? To use the technical jargon, why not advocate a principled, pluralistic ontology?

ART IN PURSUIT OF WISDOM: A PRACTICAL PEDAGOGY

A principled, pluralistic ontology refers to the notion that all cultural traditions take for granted certain primary or first principles, principles that are beyond factual determination.

For example, it is beyond the issue of empirical fact to determine if people are naturally good (Modernism) or naturally subject to folly (Conservatism); whether crime is the result of ignorance (Classicism) or capable of being based in malicious intent (Christianity); that the universe is eternal (Classicism) or created (Christianity), purposeful (Confucianism) or purposeless (Postmodern). These dichotomies are real, since arguments can be made for each of these choices, and reasonable and empirical evidence can be rallied to sway convictions. But ultimately, a choice, a judgment, a leap of faith, is inescapable.

For example, we have already seen that Modernism takes for granted that the key to human dignity and freedom is aesthetic taste, that reality conforms to our perceptions. It also assumes that an enlightened humanity will naturally be good, and that crime is the result of ignorance or social deprivation. It embraces the pursuit of facts allegedly free from considerations of ultimate purpose. But these preferences constitute a teleology and cosmology dedicated to the notion of aesthetic taste. It is maintained that facts exist, but any attempt to construct out of them a goal, a purpose, is subject to personal vision. Indeed, just as fine art conforms to our personal vision, Kant argues that nature and ethics conform to our thoughts as well.

Correspondingly, the Postmodernists take for granted that aesthetic taste is nothing but a mask for power. Consequently, they embrace a social teleology where all visions of nature, culture, and art are deemed merely expressions of power.

To the point, all cultural traditions, including Modernism and Postmodernism, embody certain first principles that can neither be empirically proven nor deemed inevitable. Those first principles result in cultural traditions that have definite and distinct characters.

That does not mean, however, that these cultures must be belligerent. Nor does it follow that, since we have to select which first principles we hold dear in forming a culture, those selections are arbitrary. That selection can be an informed judgment rather than mere opinion; it can reflect a careful consideration of the evidence. It can be seen as proof for the necessity of freedom, and for the propriety of preferring a particular House of Life. For example, we ought to respect Buddhists, Christians, Victorians, and Classicists, since their first principles can neither be deemed inescapable nor unfounded. And thank goodness for that.

But what then of those cultures that embrace totalitarian principles? What then of the Postmodernists and their excessive relatives, the Stalinists and the Nazis? What then of those traditions that value the triumph of the will? It is here that a pluralistic ontology must come to some singular conclusions. Lacking any absolutes, then a pluralistic vision of culture is incapable of distinguishing barbarism from civility and--deconstructs.

FOR THE LOVE OF BEAUTY

A pluralistic ontology is intellectually inescapable; first principles can reasonably differ. What then of cultures that advocate racism, slavery, or totalitarianism? Can we justifiably distinguish between those cultures and others? Can we justifiably prefer culture over barbarism?

Those who believe in beauty believe in ideals. And, those who believe in ideals take for granted that the facts of culture are better than the facts of life. How then do we justify a preference for the facts of culture? By recognizing that there are, I think, two first principles that are inescapable, or rather, precious: that no one can doubt that they think and live. Given that, then those traditions that deny freedom of conscience and the sanctity of life are unconscionable. In other words, it makes perfectly good sense to argue that civility and barbarism are not competing assertions of first principles, but rather, that they differ in kind and in quality. It makes perfectly good sense to deny barbaric and totalitarian "cultures."

So, any individual or group that advocates, say, slavery, rape, or forced belief, is not civil; it is barbaric and ought to be seen as such. Postmodernism notwithstanding, it is not culture that oppresses, but barbarism. Murder might be a fact of life, but it cannot be a fact of culture. So any "culture" that advocates murder is not really a culture. It is barbarism masquerading as such. A murderous culture is an oxymoron.

We might close with a quote from the renowned curator at the Museum of Fine Arts in Boston, Ananda Coomaraswamy (*Christian and Oriental Philosophy of Art* (1956) 30:

The study of art, if it is to have any cultural value, will demand...in the first place an understanding and acceptance of the whole point of view from which the necessity for the work arose, and in the second place to bringing to life in ourselves of the form in which the artist conceived the work and by which he judged it....The student of art, if he is to do more than accumulate facts, must also sacrifice himself: the wider the scope of his study in time and space, the more must he cease to be a provincial, the more he must universalize himself, whatever may be his own temperament and training.

Students of art must not only sacrifice themselves; they might also renew themselves. By rediscovering beauty, the ethical life is renewed. In discovering that a wide variety of humane first principles are possible, cosmopolitanism is achieved; by discovering that adherence to a particular cultural vision is more than merely arbitrary, then the love of beauty is consummated.

A practical pedagogy of teaching the fine arts is this:

1. Art, even aesthetic art, embodies an understanding of life; works of art objectify cultural wisdom. Therefore, teaching the fine arts focuses on searching for the wisdom embodied in a particular work of art.

2. The teacher should teach the work of art's vision of life, develop an awareness of the necessity of the work, and nurture an understanding of the first principles involved.

3. The student should understand that those principles are the substance of wisdom, the splendor of which is called beauty.

4. In teaching that there are many manifestations of beauty, the teacher need point out that they all become insignificant if we fail to distinguish culture from barbarism.

5. By cultivating a love of beauty, the ethical life is renewed.

TEACHING BUSINESS ETHICS TO
UNDERGRADUATE MANAGEMENT STUDENTS

Laurence J. Quick
School of Business
Illinois Benedictine College

INTRODUCTION

Ethical decision making in business settings can be difficult. Teaching undergraduate management students the value of ethical decision making can be very difficult, particularly when one is not a professional moral philosopher. In the face of such difficulty should management professors simply ignore ethics when teaching their courses?

In spite of the difficulty, I believe quite strongly that business ethics should become an integral part of every management course. These management courses include management principles, human resource management, international management, strategic management, production management, and small business management.

How does a management professor introduce ethics into each of these courses? How intensive should the ethics coverage be? How does a faculty member who was not trained in moral philosophy approach this task?

THE MODEL

I regularly tell my management students that to get through life effectively one needs an accurate road map. In business ethics such a road map may be referred to as a paradigm.

To provide management students with a paradigm, I have developed Exhibit A: A Managerial Model for Ethical Decision Making. While this model is far from being the ultimate paradigm, I do believe that it can serve a useful purpose. Let us briefly consider this model.

The model divides ethical decision making in business settings into four categories:

1. Decisions involving the maintenance of natural human rights (Type R-high objectivity)
2. Decisions involving fraud[1] (Type F-high objectivity)
3. Decisions involving the distribution of surplus corporate wealth (Type W-moderate to low subjectivity)
4. Decisions involving fairness in exchange (Type E-moderate to low subjectivity)

Note also that Exhibit A associates each of the four basic decision types with significant or less significant human rights implications or consequences. Type R decisions often have significant human rights consequences. Types F, W and E usually have less significant human rights consequences. Examples of these types of business decisions include whether or not to declare corporate dividends, price setting, income tax reporting, employee tuition reimbursement, and the size of employee bonuses.

Deontological ethical theory is the ethical theory that claims that the moral agent ought always to act in a way that is consistent with the moral agent's pre-existing moral duty. For example, if a moral agent believes that the Ten Commandments are God's moral law and ought always be obeyed, then the Ten Commandments create for this moral agent a pre-existing moral duty. When in the future the moral agent is confronted with an opportunity to steal, deontological ethical theory requires that the moral agent be faithful to his pre-existing moral duty not to steal.

In arriving at an agreement on what constitutes the basic set of natural human rights as the U.N. General Assembly did (see Appendix), thinking men and women by this agreement create a pre-existing moral duty. That is, all those men and women who have agreed to respect a specific set of human rights, have created for themselves in the future, a pre-existing moral duty to respect those rights for all persons. Deontological ethical theory requires fidelity to a pre-existing moral duty.

The right side of Exhibit A identifies two classes of business decisions (Types W and E) that are less objective in their nature, and are well suited to a more subjective utilitarian ethical theory. Utilitarian ethical theory is the theory that states that one ought always to act in such a way that the happiness of all concerned is maximized. Utilitarian ethical theory assesses the moral character of an intended action, in light of the intended action's projected consequences on all who are likely to be affected by the intended action.

This essay contends that it is improper to claim that ethical decision making in business settings is totally subjective. Rather, it is more appropriate to distinguish two major classes (or areas) of ethical business decisions:

1. Those business decisions involving the maintenance of natural human rights[2] (high objectivity)
2. Those business decisions involving the distribution of surplus corporate wealth (moderate subjectivity)

Let us consider the first class of business decisions--those involving the maintenance or deprivation of natural human rights. Such business decisions are often critical to human health. As a result, this class of business decisions is subject to a high degree of objectivity. That is to say, the personal values and preferences of the manager do not determine whether a business decision in this category is ethical or unethical. If a manager knowingly makes a business decision that has a significant probability of depriving even one corporate stakeholder of even one natural human right, then such a business decision is unethical, regardless of the manager's personal values and preferences.

An ethics decision model which seeks always to protect natural human rights is deontological in its nature. That is to say, such an ethics decision model seeks to honor a pre-existing moral duty.

Let us now consider the second class (or area) of business decisions--those business decisions involving the distribution of surplus corporate wealth. Managerial decisions involving the distribution of corporate wealth frequently are not critical to human health. Often these business decisions do not immediately threaten the preservation of natural human rights. As a result, surplus wealth decisions involve a moderate degree of subjectivity. That is to say, women and men of goodwill can hold substantial differences of opinion on how such corporate wealth ought to be distributed to the various corporate stakeholders. Because of their nature, decisions about the proper distribution of surplus wealth lend themselves to a more subjective utilitarian assessment.

The lower portion of Exhibit A presents a limited number of principles to guide business decision makers. These principles will hopefully serve as useful guides for managers. While some of these principles have been defined in Exhibit A, two principles have not. These two principles are:

1. The Golden Rule (Negative Version)
2. The Golden Rule (Positive Version)

The Golden Rule (Negative Version) has been articulated by Confucius as "What you do not wish done to yourself, do not do to others." The Golden Rule (Positive Version) may be expressed as "Do unto others as you would have them do unto you." I believe that both of these versions of the Golden Rule are examples of Immanuel Kant's Categorical Imperative, "Always act in such a way that you can also will that the maxim of your action should become a universal law."

Although defined in Exhibit A, another principle meriting discussion is The Light of Day Test. The Light of Day Test can be expressed as follows "Make no decision and take no action that you would not want exposed to the light of day." That is to say, make no decision and take no action which you would not want revealed publicly. A qualification to the Light of Day Test is in order. There are sets of business information and business decisions which are perfectly ethical, yet which should not be subject to public revelation. Such decisions and information involve competitive strategies, individual employee salaries, and special production processes. Business decisions which should be subjected to the Light of Day Test include the payment of bribes and kickbacks, deceptive sales practices, price gouging, and decisions to market unsafe products.

USING THE MODEL

Exhibit A - A Managerial Model for Ethical Decision Making presents eight suggested ethical principles. These principles are:

1. The Golden Rule (Negative Version)
2. The Golden Rule (Positive Version)
3. The Light of Day Test
4. Consistency with the U.N. International Declaration of Human Rights
5. The Profits Versus Rights Conflict Principle
6. Utilitarianism
7. The Minimum Distribution Principle
8. The Distributive Justice Principle

When a management decision maker is confronted with a problem that involves ethical issues, the decision maker must do two things. First, the management decision maker must classify the decision into one of the four categories presented in Exhibit A. Second, the management decision maker must apply all of the applicable ethical principles presented in Exhibit A for the relevant decision category. A few examples are in order. Let us begin with Type R decisions.

Suppose a chemical manufacturer knowingly or unknowingly pollutes the local water supply with toxic waste. Natural human rights have been violated. The surrounding community using the polluted water has had one of its natural human needs denied--the need for safe drinking water.

Consider the employer who removes safety guards from production machinery to increase productivity. As a result, several employees loose their fingers. Again a natural human right has been violated as a natural human need has been denied satisfaction, that is, the right to physical safety.

Whenever any human being is denied the legitimate satisfaction of a natural human need,[3] one of their natural human rights has been violated. Whenever a natural human right has been violated an injustice has occurred. The injustice may be committed intentionally or unintentionally. If it has been committed intentionally then moral culpability rests with the agent. The injustice may be perpetrated by an individual, a group, an organization, a government, or a society.

If one accepts the claim that natural human rights have always existed for *all* human beings, currently exist for *all* human beings and will exist for *all* human beings, then Type R decisions are well suited to a deontological approach to ethical theory. That is to say, when a business decision maker is faced with a decision having likely human rights consequences, a deontological approach would require adherence by the business decision maker to a pre-existing moral duty. No business decision should be made for which a significant probability exists that even one natural human right of even one human being will be violated. In other words, all human beings have a pre-existing moral duty not to deprive one another of natural human rights. Such a pre-existing moral duty comes into existence when business decision makers agree on a specific set of natural human rights, and pledge to honor such rights for *all* corporate stakeholders in the future. Forbearance from fraudulent business practices can also be added to the list of pre-existing moral duties.

When confronted with a Type R decision the management decision maker, in the opinion of this author, should adhere to each of the five ethical principles listed at the bottom of the second column in Exhibit A. The management decision maker should assure herself that the intended course of action is consistent with the U.N. International Declaration of Human Rights. The intended course of action should never sacrifice (for increased corporate profits) the human rights of even a single corporate stakeholder. The management decision maker should undertake no action that the decision maker would not want inflicted upon herself. The management decision maker should have no reservations about exposing the decision made to public scrutiny should such exposure be required by legal authorities. Finally, if relevant, the management decision maker should select a course of action of which the decision maker would like to be the beneficiary. If the course of action is not consistent with any one of these five Type R ethical principles, then the proposed course of action is most likely an unethical one.

It was previously asserted that forbearance from fraudulent business practices can also be added to the list of pre-existing moral duties. Type F business decisions include but are not limited to sales practices, income tax reporting, financial statement presentation, and labor practices. In the author's opinion all human beings have a natural human right to be free from fraudulent business practices. Let us consider an example involving sales practices.

Suppose Jan Smith reads an advertisement in the newspaper for a used automobile which is being offered for sale by Greasy 2 Corporation. Johnson, a salesmen for Greasy 2, asserts that the 1992 Pontiac Grand Am for sale has been owned by a school teacher who has driven the auto less than 40,000 miles. Smith notes that the odometer reads 39,554 miles. Relying on Johnsons's statement and the stated mileage on the odometer, Smith purchases the car for $8,000. Within two weeks Smith starts experiencing serious mechanical problems with the auto. She is informed by her mechanic that both the engine and the transmission will have to be replaced at a cost of $2,500.

In reality, the 1992 Grand Am had been purchased from a rental car company with accumulated mileage of 92,000. As a result of the fraudulent sales practices conducted by Greasy 2 management and its sales representative, Smith paid $6,000 more for the auto than its "true" market value.

Which ethical principles should have been followed by Greasy 2 management and its salesman? What if the situation were reversed, and Johnson was looking for a used automobile? Would Johnson want to be lied to by an auto salesman? Would Johnson want to purchase an auto with an odometer understated by 52,000 miles? Would Johnson like his misrepresentation to Smith about the auto's previous owner brought to light through investigative television journalism? If a business decision maker is contemplating a decision that violates the Golden Rule (Negative Version), the Golden Rule (Positive Version), or the Light of Day Test, then the contemplated business decision is most likely an unethical one.

Many business decisions can be grouped into one of two broad classifications:

1. Those decisions that likely will deprive a corporate stakeholder of something that the corporate stakeholder owns or is entitled to.
2. Those decisions involving the distribution of corporate assets.

For those business decisions that will deprive one or more stakeholders of that to which they are legitimately entitled, a deontological approach to ethical decision making is appropriate. That is to say, management decision makers have a pre-existing moral duty to honor *all* the human rights of *all* corporate stakeholders. These business decisions are the Type F and Type R decisions presented in Exhibit A.

The second broad classification of business decisions involves the distribution or allocation of corporate resources. These are the Type W and Type E business decisions presented in Exhibit A. To "fairly" allocate corporate resources, the application of utilitarian ethical theory is most appropriate. That is to say, the management decision maker ought to distribute surplus corporate wealth in a way that maximizes the utility (happiness or satisfaction) of all corporate stakeholders who deserve consideration.[4]

Let us consider an example involving a Type W decision. Suppose firm has earned $10 million of unexpected profits. How can this $10 million best be distributed to corporate stakeholders? Should all of the $10 million be given to stockholders in the form of dividends? Should some of this profit be distributed in the form of executive bonuses or employee profit sharing? Should employees be given added fringe benefits?

Assume that the disposition of this $10 million must be approved by the firm's board of directors. How can the board allocate the $10 million in a way which will maximize the happiness of all concerned? Before addressing this question a few items need clarification.

In the opinion of the author, the focus of attention must be on need satisfaction. Satisfied needs produce human happiness. Happiness cannot be sought directly. Therefore, in applying utilitarian ethical theory, the goal is to satisfy the greatest number of human needs beginning with those needs that are most pressing.

The application of utilitarian ethical theory should be democratic (i.e. participative) in its application. How can the board know which pattern of wealth distribution will satisfy the greatest number of human needs, covering first those that are most important for stakeholder welfare? One approach would be to ask representatives from each group of corporate stakeholders for their suggestions. In this manner a consensus on a fair allocation might be arrived at, or at least approached.

In allocating surplus corporate wealth, each of the five principles listed at the bottom of the third column in Exhibit A should be addressed. Is the selected allocation pattern one that the Board would *not* mind being exposed to public scrutiny? Is the selected allocation pattern one that the Board members should like for themselves, if they were to be members of each stakeholder group? Has the allocation pattern satisfied the minimum distribution principle, namely, no corporate stakeholder should have so much that another has too little? Will the surplus corporate wealth be distributed in a way that fairly compensates stakeholders on the basis of their contribution to the creation of the surplus corporate wealth? Having honored each of these ethical principles for Type W decisions, do we believe that the proposed allocation pattern will result in the greatest need satisfaction for all relevant corporate stakeholders? If this turns out to be the case, then it is possible that the greatest happiness for the greatest number may be realized.

At this point, I would like to state my belief in the impossibility of ever knowing precisely and with certitude that the greatest happiness for the greatest number has been realized. To do this would require the development of an accurate "happiness meter" which would have to be connected to psyches of each stakeholder affected by a resource allocation decision. Even if such a device could be created, resource allocation can occur only once. Resource allocation is not an experiment that can be repeated and varied again and again under laboratory conditions.

The best a management decision maker can hope for is a participative process of resource allocation that each group of corporate stakeholders considers fair. One never knows whether one has selected the "optimal" residence to purchase. The application of utilitarian ethical theory necessitates imprecision and subjective probabilities.

Type E decisions include but are not limited to price setting, labor force compensation, and the payment of bribes and kickbacks. Let us consider an example involving employee compensation.

Exhibit A makes a distinction between essential employee compensation (a Type R decision) and labor force compensation (a Type E decision). Essential employee compensation may be defined as that level of compensation necessary for an employee to survive as a healthy human being. The level of compensation essential to a healthy existence will vary from one culture to another and will also vary over time. In the author's opinion, all employers have a moral obligation to pay their employees a "living wage." Only in very unusual circumstances might the payment of a "living wage" be impossible. Certainly U.S. firms operating in Mexico's Maquiladora district can afford to pay Mexican workers more than $2 per hour in addition to providing a basic benefits package.

Assume that Flying High Airlines is a large U.S. airline carrying passengers all across North America. In 1990 Flying High's CEO earned over $18 million. Flight attendants for Flying High earned a starting salary of $12,000 per year. Salaries for all flight attendants had been frozen for the past five years by the CEO as a cost containment measure. Which ethical principles should be applied by Flying High's CEO when setting compensation levels? Exhibit A lists four relevant ethical principles:

1. The Golden Rule (Negative Versions)
2. The Golden Rule (Positive Version
3. The Light of Day Test
4. The Minimum Distribution Principle

If the situation were reversed and Flying High's CEO were a flight attendant, would he like his starting salary to be $12,000 per year? Would he like the firm's CEO to be earning a compensation package 1500 times greater than his own? ($18,000,000 ÷ $12,000) Would he like his salary frozen by his employer for five years?

The Minimum Distribution Principle states that no corporate stakeholder should have so much that another has too little. Although flight attendants earning $12,000 per year will probably not go hungry, fairness would dictate that a large portion of the CEO's $18,000,000 compensation package be reallocated to flight attendant salaries. Finally, an annual compensation ratio of 1500:1 is a statistic Flying High's CEO would most likely not wish to have exposed to the "light of day."

PRINCIPLES[5] VERSUS RULES[6]

The model of ethical decision making presented in this essay has been formulated in terms of "guiding principles" rather than "rules." I deliberately chose the term "principle" because of its open-ended character.

Long ago Aristotle warned against seeking inappropriately rigid standards in the field of moral philosophy. In his *Nicomachean Ethics*, he stated that his own "discussion will be adequate if it has as much clearness as the subject-matter admits, for precision is not to be sought for alike in all discussion." In ethical matters, "to indicate the truth roughly and in outline" represents no shortcoming.[7] Forcing ethical issues into a rigid, mathematic-like mold would constitute a distortion of the nature of those issues.

Hence, it is my contention that ethical decision making, like a work of art, can be discussed most profitably in terms of principles and not rules. Rules are applied in an "all or nothing" fashion. When rules come into conflict, at least one of them must be abandoned or altered. Rules need little interpretation when applied to specific cases. Principles, by contrast, guide our thinking in a different manner. Principles need to be applied thoughtfully to particular circumstances. When principles clash, none of them need to be abandoned. Rather the clash creates a need for the principles relevant to the situation to be ranked and prioritized.

My position is that no model of ethical decision making should be interpreted as a device used to determine matters of right or wrong, good or evil in a mechanical fashion. I sincerely hope that the model discussed here has yielded some degree of enlightenment. Properly understood, the model represents a guide in making ethical business decisions. It is not intended to replace the need to think carefully about particular situations as they arise.[8]

Notes

1. Business fraud is here defined as language or behavior that is intended to deceive one or more parties to a business transaction.

2. A natural human right may be defined as a valid claim to the legitimate satisfaction of a natural human need. Natural human needs include but are not limited to the need for an adequate supply of food, water, clothing, liberty, education, physical safety, human relationships, clean air, clean water, and clean earth. See Appendix I for a comprehensive summary of natural human rights.

3. A natural human need is defined as a need with which all human beings are born.

4. Surplus corporate wealth may be defined as the excess of assets over liabilities on the firm's balance sheet.

5. A principle is here defined as a desirable or necessary method of operation.

6. A rule is here defined as a rigid, inflexible requirement.

7. Aristotle, "Nicomachean Ethics," *The Basic Works of Aristotle*. Richard McKeon, ed., New York: Random House, 1941, p. 936.

8. These observations are the work of Dr. Joseph F. Biel, Department of Philosophy, Illinois Benedictine College, Lisle, Illinois.

Exhibit A: A Mangerial Model for Ethical Decision Making

Ethical Decisions

Deontological Approach*

Decisions Involving Fraud - Significant Human Rights Implications (Type F)

Examples
1. Sales Practices
2. Income Tax Reporting
3. Financial Statement Presentation
4. Labor practices

Decision Making Principles
1. The Golden Rule (Negative)
2. The Golden Rule (Positive)
3. The Light of Day Test- Refrain from decisions and actions that one would not wish exposed to the light of day

*Fidelity to a pre-existing moral duty
**Collective utility maximazation subject to the minimum distribution principle
***An implication is defined here as a consequence

Decisions Involving the Maintenance of Natural Human Rights - Significant Human Rights Implications*(Type R)**

Examples
1. Employee Health and Safety
2. Environmental Pollution
3. Storage of Explosive Materials
4. Consumer Safety
5. Essential Compensation
6. Essential Health Care Benefits
7. Emerg. Charitable Contributions
8. Access to Promotion
9. Stakeholder Privacy
10. Sexual Harassment
11. Theft

Decison Making Principles
1. Consistency with United Nations International Declaration of Human Rights
2. Profits vs. Rights Conflict Principle - Whenever a conflict exists between human rights and corporate profits, corporate profits must suffer
3. Golden Rule (Positive Version)
4. Golden Rule (Negative Version)
5. Light of Day Test

Utilitarian Approach**

Decisions Involving the Distribution of Surplus Corporate Wealth - Less Significant Human Rights Implications (Type W)

Examples
1. Dividend Distributions
2. Executive Bonuses
3. Employee Bonuses
4. Profit Sharing Distributions
5. Employee Benefits Excluding Essential Employee Health Care
6. Non-emergency Charitable Contributions

Decision Making Principles
1. Utilitarianism- Seek the greatest happiness for the greatest number of corporate stakeholders
2. Minimum Distribution Principle- No corporate stakeholder should have so much that another has too little
3. Distributive Justice Principle- Surplus corporate wealth should be distributed based on the corporate stakeholder's contribution to the creation of that wealth
4. Golden Rule (Positive Version)
5. Light of Day Test

Decisions Involving Fairness in Exchange - Less Significant Human Rights Implications (Type E)

Examples
1. Price Setting
2. Labor Force Compensation
3. Payments of Bribes and Kickbacks

Decision Making Principles
1. Golden Rule (Negative Version)
2. Golden Rule (Positive Version)
3. Light of Day Test
4. Minimum Distribution Principle

Appendix

Second Yearbook of the United Nations
June 30, 1947 to September 21, 1948

Draft Declaration
The text of the draft Declaration as forwarded to the seventh session
of the Council was as follows:

DRAFT INTERNATIONAL DECLARATION
OF HUMAN RIGHTS

Preamble

Whereas recognition of the inherent dignity and of the equal and
inalienable rights of all members of the human family is the foundation
of freedom, justice and peace in the world; and

Whereas disregard and contempt for human rights resulted, before
and during the Second World War, in barbarous acts which outraged
the conscience of mankind and made it apparent that the fundamental
freedoms were one of the supreme issues of the conflict; and

Whereas it is essential, if mankind is not to be compelled as a last
resort to rebel against tyranny and oppression, that human rights should
be protected by a regime of law; and

Whereas the peoples of the United Nations have in the Charter
determined to reaffirm faith in fundamental human rights and in the
dignity and worth of the human person and to promote social progress
and better standards of life in larger freedom; and

Whereas Member States have pledged themselves to achieve, in cooperation with the Organization, the promotion of universal respect for
and observance of human rights and fundamental freedoms; and

Whereas a common understanding of these rights and freedoms is
of the greatest importance for the full realization of this pledge,

Now therefore the General Assembly

Proclaims this Declaration of Human Rights as a common standard
of achievement for all peoples and all nations, to the end that every
individual and every organ of society, keeping this Declaration
constantly in mind, shall strive by teaching and education to promote
respect for these rights and freedoms and by progressive measures,
national and international, to secure their universal and effective

recognition and observance, both among the peoples of Member States themselves and among the peoples of territories under their jurisdiction.

Article 1

All human beings are born free and equal in dignity and rights. They are endowed by nature with reason and conscience, and should act towards one another in a spirit of brotherhood.

Article 2

Everyone is entitled to all the rights and freedoms set forth in this Declaration, without distinction of any kind, such as race, colour, sex, language, religion, political or other opinion, property or other status, or national or social origin.

Article 3

Everyone has the right to life, liberty and security of person.

Article 4

1. No one shall be held in slavery or involuntary servitude.

2. No one shall be subjected to torture or to cruel, inhuman or degrading treatment or punishment.

Article 5

Everyone has the right to recognition everywhere as a person before the law.

Article 6

All are equal before the law and are entitled without any discrimination to equal protection of the law against any discrimination in violation of this Declaration and against any incitement to such discrimination.

Article 7

No one shall be subjected to arbitrary arrest or detention.

Article 8

In the determination of his rights and obligations and of any criminal charge against him, everyone is entitled in full equality to a fair hearing by an independent and impartial tribunal.

Article 9

1. Everyone charged with a penal offence has the right to be presumed innocent until proven guilty according to law in a public trial at which he has had all the guarantees necessary for his defence.

2. No one shall be held guilty of any offence on account of any act or omission which did not constitute an offence, under national or

international law, at the time when it was committed.
Article 10
No one shall be subjected to unreasonable interference with his privacy, family, home, correspondence, or reputation.
Article 11
1. Everyone has the right to freedom of movement and residence within the borders of each State.
2. Everyone has the right to leave any country, including his own.
Article 12
1. Everyone has the right to seek and be granted, in other countries, asylum from persecution.
2. Prosecutions genuinely arising from non-political crimes or from acts contrary to the purposes and principles of the United Nations do not constitute persecution.
Article 13
No one shall be arbitrarily deprived of his nationality or denied the right to change his nationality.
Article 14
1. Men and women of full age have the right to marry and to found a family and are entitled to equal rights as to marriage.
2. Marriage shall be entered into only with the full consent of both intending spouses.
3. The family is the natural and fundamental group of society and is entitled to protection.
Article 15
1. Everyone has the right to own property alone as well as in association with others.
2. No one shall be arbitrarily deprived of his property.
Article 16
Everyone has the right to freedom of thought, conscience and religion; this right includes freedom to change his religion or belief, and freedom, either alone or in community with others and in public or private, to manifest his religion or belief in teaching, practice, worship and observance.
Article 17
Everyone has the right to freedom of opinion and expression; this right includes freedom to hold opinions without interference and to see, receive and impart information and ideas through any media and

regardless of frontiers.
Article 18
Everyone has the right to freedom of assembly and association.
Article 19
1. Everyone has the right to take part in the government of his country, directly or through his freely chosen representatives.
2. Everyone has the right of access to public employment in his country.
3. Everyone has the right to a government which conforms to the will of the people.
Article 20
Everyone, as a member of society, has the right to social security and is entitled to the realization, through national effort and international co-operation, and in accordance with the organization and resources of each State, of the economic, social and cultural rights set out below.
Article 21
1. Everyone has the right to work, to just and favourable conditions of work and pay and to protection against unemployment.
2. Everyone has the right to equal pay for equal work.
3. Everyone is free to form and to join trade unions for the protection of his interests.
Article 22
1. Everyone has the right to a standard of living, including food, clothing, housing and medical care, and to social services, adequate for the health and well-being of himself and his family and to security in the event of unemployment, sickness, disability, old age or other lack of livelihood in circumstances beyond his control.
2. Mother and child have the right to special care and assistance.
Article 23
1. Everyone has the right to education. Elementary and fundamental education shall be free and compulsory and there shall be equal access on the basis of merit to higher education.
2. Education shall be directed to the full development of the human personality, to strengthening respect for human rights and fundamental freedoms and to combating the spirit of intolerance and hatred against other nations and against racial and religious groups everywhere.

Article 24

Everyone has the right to rest and leisure.

Article 25

Everyone has the right to participate in the cultural life of the community, to enjoy the arts and to share in scientific advancement.

Article 26

Everyone is entitled to a good social and international order in which the rights and freedoms set out in this Declaration can be fully realized.

Article 27

1. Everyone has duties to the community which enables him freely to develop his personality.

2. In the exercise of his rights, everyone shall be subject only to such limitations as are necessary to secure due recognition and respect for the rights of others and the requirements of morality, public order and the general welfare in a democratic society.

Article 28

Nothing in this Declaration shall imply the recognition of the right of any State or person to engage in any activity aimed at the destruction of any of the rights and freedoms prescribed herein.

Note. The Commission has not considered the following article since measures of implementation were not discussed in its third session:

Everyone has the right, either individually, or in association with others, to petition or to communicate with the public authorities of the State of which he is a national or in which he resides, or with the United Nations.

MORAL DEVELOPMENT AND FRESHMAN STUDIES

Bruce W. Stuart
Department of History
Concordia College

Principia: Foundational Study in the Liberal Arts...is designed to...engage students and faculty in the investigation of issues indigenous to the liberal arts and its emphasis in value-reflective inquiry; introduce students to the habits of mind and disposition that mark the liberally educated person and to the skills required in reflective analysis of values-centered problems.[1]

In the decade during which Principia has been part of the required Freshman Core at Concordia College, the course has drawn faculty and students into disciplined conversation through classroom discussion and expository exercises. More than 5,000 participants have addressed classical and contemporary "texts" (including musical pieces and films) which provide the literary and artistic bases upon which to develop a "communal venture of inquiry" into "perennial problems...,chosen for their enduring value and their interdisciplinary and values-centered character."

As might be imagined, the first encounters of Midwestern frosh with the literary remains of those whom Bernard Knox calls "The Oldest Dead White European Males,"[2] the polemics of Thoreau and Martin Luther King, Jr., the wit and rage of Kate Chopin and Margaret Atwood, and the complexities of both the academic career and the scientific achievement of molecular biologist, Barbara McClintock, have often prompted perplexed outbursts: "What is Principia? What am I doing in this class? What does this stuff have to do with my life, anyway?" As they swim upstream against the queries of Plato's *Apology* and resist in the *Crito* blandishments of Socrates' use of a "parent-child" metaphor to justify his own submission to "home-town authorities," students, who are but recently removed from home-towns and authorities, wonder aloud: "What is in this for us? Why do we hafta read that...?" And faculty dutifully respond by lauding the classics and critical thinking, by citing the values of "a life well-read" and modeling the hectic life reading papers; by leading discussion to culminate in yet another essay that will be snipped from the late-night, recalcitrant printer. And so it goes....

As the Principia faculty "committee of the whole" has directed itself in thematic concerns for "Justice" and "Freedom and Authority" and will soon focus on "The Examined Life," we exhort our student-colleagues to read critically, to discuss civilly (while also expressing universal reason and personal passion), and to write cogently (in styles somehow formal and also colloquial). Such exhortation partly represents faculty advocacy of the contemplative life and those intellectual virtues conducive to satisfactory discourse among the scholarly. Teachers encourage among the students virtuosity in study and excellence in conversation about what is learned. Faculty members seek more, however, much more than the initiation of their students into privileged intellectualist pursuits.[3] They seek also to inculcate the "habits of mind" to inquire, deliberate, speak and act in the wholeness of a life which flourishes--to express the goodness of a life well-lived even beyond the confines of academic halls and cloistered dormitories.

In a word, character formation or moral development is also presupposed as part of the working agenda of this "value-centered inquiry." While primary attention is given to what passes for contemporary intellectual virtues--capacities to read and argue discursively, ability to observe and report, talents to imagine and create--Principia also gives occasion for personal growth that is essentially moral in its nature. More specifically: Principia mandates a reflective, dialogical encounter with textual exemplars of several moral traditions--with faculty expectations that students will discern much that is personally relevant, cognitively and emotionally satisfying in the religious, cultural and intellectual heritage that has shaped their own lives.

Student contact with philosophical essays, paintings, theological disputation, and utopian literature should bring to mind numerous facets of the conventional morality in which they are enmeshed. What is more, most students, most of the time, will reaffirm the customary conduct of their lives, the traditional moral principles of home and church, the mores of the communities with which they are most familiar.[4] The course-work encounter, however, will most certainly lead beyond a reaffirmation of the customary patterns of the student's local tradition, beyond spontaneous expressions that somehow fit into the familiar rules that were not left behind on registration day.[5] In the Principia process--as students learn of the ideals, commitments, and modes of thought of people who powerfully portray their own experiences, reflect values, and embody choices much at variance with the students'--the participants find themselves caught up in a struggle for self-knowledge and personal direction in the conduct of their own lives.[6] They face, often in surprise and dismay, challenges to the moral traditions which they have taken for granted. The familiar circumstances of reading assignments and engaging in classroom discussions become discomfiting as the half-willing student is pushed to self-examination when the conventionalities of even her young life are confronted by novel alternatives that prompt intellectual uncertainty, the trauma of moral dilemmas, and existential anguish.

In brief, what faculty blithely refer to as "a common intellectual experience in the liberal arts at the beginning of a student's career,"[7] students meet as something quite disturbing. From their perspective the course constitutes a "shaking of the foundations" which occurs ironically amidst a process that appeared to be merely conventional, like going through all those texts and talks of the student's high school career. In this new college context, in fact, Principia marks the end of one stage of the student's education and initiates a new stage in the person's life-way. From the viewpoint of the faculty, the shakiness of the student's life that may manifest itself through encounter with texts or in the 3:30 p.m. dialogue has not been generated as an ironic by-product of the Principia process. Principia's conventional appearance has deceived the student; the course is intended to touch the student's life and affect it deeply.

John Kekes in *The Examined Life* suggests a good way to construe Principia. The shakedown that occasions the course expresses a normal, maybe a necessary, step that each participant takes toward a form of self-knowledge, wherein she both interprets her place within a moral tradition and evaluates facets of that tradition in terms of their significance for meeting individual needs and desires.[8] In Principia, the value-reflective inquiry "shakes foundations" so that participants might determine for themselves a clear, realistic description both of the traditions out of which they have emerged and the circumstances in which they currently live.   Finally class members may make crucial decisions concerning the appropriation of the ideals and values which contribute to the flourishing of their own lives.[9]

Kekes, reviewing Montaigne's *Essays*, summarizes this moral task of self-description and evaluation. "First, we must take from our moral tradition ideals, adopt them to our character and circumstances, and forge out of them our individual conceptions of a good life. This requires us to assess the importance of various ideals and commit ourselves to their realization....Second, we must make ourselves into the kind of agents who are capable of living according to their ideals."[10]

Student encounters with several commonly assigned texts illustrate how "shaking the foundations" of conventional morality can prompt self-examination, lead to a realistic appraisal of circumstances, and spur action to realize moral commitments. In *Man's Search For Meaning*, Viktor Frankl's portrayal of Nazi concentration camps confronts students with a graphic description of inhumanity, evil and extreme suffering. Frankl's sparse prose depicts systemic injustice, torture, and suicide.   Students are imaginatively drawn into the indignities of camplife where cigarettes symbolize life, theft is normal, selfishness is typical and altruism rare. The text evokes "the normalcy" of the camp, but students feel its hellacious circumstance as a challenge to their normal views of communal existence. Reading what Frankl and his fellow-prisoners handled, what they experienced, Principia participants ask, "What would I have done? Would I have stolen, lied, abandoned my friends, used violence?" Seeing that Frankl discerned meaning in suffering, expressed purposes greater than mere survival, and somehow managed to cherish moments of memory and hope, students ponder the goodness of family life, the value of professional duties, the taste of food, the sound of music, the reality of daydreams and the blessings of love.

In another part of the course, Martin Luther in "Christian Liberty," an ethical-theological essay, not only challenges students to consider predestinarian features of Christianity but also projects the strenuous demand of an ethic of radical service to the "neighbor in need." Many students who have learned at home and church that altruism is a dimension of the Christian life find in Luther's essay a too radical vision of self-sacrifice, and they resist exhortations to "burn themselves up" in bearing others' burdens. They ask, "Must Christians really live that way?"

Late in the course, students read Margaret Sanger's "Birth Control--A Woman's Problem or Her Parents?" which argues for a female prerogative in birth control, against the social attitudes that restricted female reproductive choices in the 1920's. While contemporary students support female primacy in reproductive matters, when the discussion invariably expands to include abortion issues, every student finds his conventional morality under fire from his classmates.[11] Henry David Thoreau's "Civil Disobedience" articulates a radical individualistic approach to freedom that differs from Luther's, and Kate Chopin's "The Story of An Hour," a biting short story, is suggestive of ambiguity, pain, and danger in a woman's liberation from her marriage. And so it goes. Students' conventional morality, their self-expressed ideals, and the normal rules that shape their daily lives are ground to grist in the Principia mill.

John Kekes' treatment of "the examined life," with its attention on each person's development of self-directing knowledge of the ideals and the circumstances which shape him and present him with possibilities for the flourishing of life, constitutes an extensive text for analyzing Principia as an occasion for the moral development of its participants.[12] If "shaking the student's foundations" to encourage self-examination and criticism of conventional morality is an integral dimension of the teacher's task within Principia, Kekes' insights will facilitate faculty evaluation of how the distinctive readings, discussions and expository assignments contribute to the process of moral discernment and activity which characterize a student's flourishing life--the well-living of a moral person.

Such an extensive analysis, however, would be most proper to a course evaluation committee and would mandate a review of the numerous sections that are taught annually; it reaches beyond my present task. For a more limited agenda, Kekes' work and his reliance on Aristotle's ethics provide a helpful resource. Kekes cites Aristotelian views on choosing ideals and manifesting freedom as self-control, in making choices of ethical ends and acting in pursuit of the life which flourishes.[13] References to *Nicomachean Ethics*, Book Three, and to Aristotle's expanded treatment of "choice," "deliberation," and "practical wisdom" in Book Six can aid our analysis of a couple of the moral development features of Principia.[14]

The pedagogy of my class emphasizes a large-group conversation among 20-25 students about the assigned texts. In rapid-fire fashion, I pose questions and make comments to elicit student responses. I re-direct remarks to assist students. I occasionally intervene to change topics. For these conversations I admonish students to two general "rules of discourse." 1. They are to represent accurately the text under consideration, that is, summarize clearly "the author's," "the other's," ideas. 2. They are to present their opinions, take a personal stance and express their own ideas on the topics.

In these informal student exchanges, I detect the "shaking foundations" and students' effort to express ideals and make personal commitments amidst ambiguity. I hear also the clash of values and--often--the deafening silences that suggest the paralysis of students' wills, their inability to act on behalf of the conventional rules of their moral traditions (even within the friendly confines of classroom conversation). I, as teacher, might feel satisfaction in observing student engagement with significant texts, rejoice in the frustration of certain of their conventional views, and even characterize the silences as "creative moments." but when the primary concern is the students' moral development, I expect more, if Principia conversation is to become "good conversation."

A good conversation in this context will not only "shake foundations" and call into question the conventional morality of the conversants; it will also direct their thought to ideals, toward the goal of living well and to the commitments and action appropriate to achieve their goal.[15] In Aristotelian terms, the conversation should be for the sake of the individual's "practical wisdom" (*phronesis*) and his deliberation (*bouleusis*) on conduct in the concrete circumstances in which he lives.[16]

The moments of conversation should contribute to each person's affirmation of distinctive goals toward which he might direct himself and so flourish, that is, live well. The speaking and the listening should also assist each person so she can use her judgment to determine appropriate means to gain her life's ends, means that are peculiar to her unique circumstances. In view of these two stipulations, the Principia conversations which "settle for" merely shaking the foundations and do not offer up visions, images, or rational descriptions of "the noble, the good, the best" life that can be lived (or dreamed or hoped for), lack possibility for moral discernment. If no parts of conversation provide opportunity for a student to exercise thought and desire and to manifest some activity toward realization of a life-goal that she deems worthy (if "working out" the way to achieve the flourishing of life is not permitted in the Principia process), the conversation itself "does not work" for moral development. *Principia should be for the sake of practical wisdom and deliberation.*

In Aristotle's view, practical wisdom is primarily concerned with one's own person and knowing what is good for oneself, so that one might do the right things.[17] Such wisdom expresses itself as the person acts for his own well- being in clear-minded assessment of the limits and opportunities which his family, his profession, his community and nature have posed for him as the ordinary circumstances of his life. Immersed in their circumstances, such wisdom prompts its practitioners to "see what is good for themselves" and to act on that basis. The practice of wisdom presupposes not only insight into the particularities of circumstance and changes in the world that is external to the person, but also insight into numerous needs and desires that are peculiar to himself. As John Kekes argues, practical wisdom not only encompasses descriptive knowledge of the facts of a situation, but also their significance, not only interpretation of moral conventions, but also their appropriateness for the individual. And wisdom includes knowledge ofthe connection between facts and circumstances, the moral tradition, moral ends and the character of the person involved.[18]

If, then, we attribute practical wisdom to someone, we will note his capacity to grasp significant facts, to discern features of his moral tradition and to realize how changing circumstances give opportunities for him to realize good for himself through his own action.   In Aristotle's terms, this person shows "the capacity of deliberating well about what is good and advantageous for oneself."[19] This person is one who can "calculate well with respect to some worthwhile end."   If one assumes the goal, deliberation is the consideration of specific modes of action which may in the particular circumstance gain the goodness of life. People "deliberate about matters which are done through our own agency," and "about things that are in our power and can be realized in action...."[20]   Accordingly, out of the personal commitment to living well, the grasping of an ideal as one's own task, emerges a significant challenge for the individual to reflect about the concrete means by which to flourish.

From this perspective that is concerned with a student's moral development, Principia conversation has two facets, presentation of worthy ideals and encouragement of deliberation.   Creating conversational space and intellectual support so that a freshman might envision and select the good life for himself--this is essential.   But ensuing conversation should also invite each person to test his renewed character in thoughtful conduct. The speaking and listening represent a public aspect of exercising judgment and acting in line with the envisioned goal. In this conversational mode, participants "work their way" from their desires and interest in specific goals (from their commitments) to choices on methods of how best to gain that which is thought good for themselves.

To be sure, the task of distinguishing between the process of appropriating specific goals for living well and acting toward those goals rather than others and the process of deliberation is complicated. (And neither John Kekes nor Aristotle has clarified every key distinction here.)[21] Indeed, it may be no more difficult for us to follow Aristotle and his commentator in these matters than it is for my Principia students to clarify the assigned texts and represent their personal views, and also to act toward life-affirming ends--all within a common conversational process in a single college course!   Nonetheless,

Aristotle's treatment emphasizes that, in deliberation, personal investigation seeks "the instruments" to enact and embody the best of life as the individual conceives the best to be.

Recall that the student is asked to respond personally to texts, to study and "work out" a commentary that is both germane to the assignment and expressive of unique insight. In comparable fashion, the individual who chooses to live well through a commitment to an ideal also directs herself to establish interpretations of the situation, self-appraisals and particular choices of action. By doing these things, she places her distinct stamp on "living the good life" *and her life flourishes with its own peculiar bent.*

If, then, a "good Principia conversation" brings specific ideals of the good life before the student who may willingly commit herself to their realization, so should the conversation be an occasion for the "ideal-fascinated person" to reflect and take steps to fulfill the ideals which now challenge her character and conduct. If a Freshman Studies course were to dare, not only to support student encounters with classical texts and to expect personal responses to the "great works of others,", but also to place before its participants the conception and the challenge of the "life well-lived" and finally to provide conversational space for each person to reflect concrete ways of realizing such worthy good--NOW THERE IS A PROBLEMATIC FOR MORAL DEVELOPMENT in any college course.

Notes

1. *An Agenda for Concordia Academic Life.* (Concordia College, Moorhead, MN, 1984), p. 22-24.

2. (New York, 1993).

3. John M. Cooper, *Reason and Human Good in Aristotle.* (Harvard University Press, Cambridge, 1975), p.144-150.

4. John Kekes, *The Examined Life.* (Associated University Press, Cranbury, NJ, 1988), p.49-51.

5. *Ibid.*, p.49.

6. *Ibid.*, p. 72-76.

7. *Agenda*, p. 23.

8. Kekes, p. 117-122.

9. *Ibid.*, p. 73-76.

10. *Ibid.*, p. 75-76.

11. Reprinted in *Principia Anthology, 1992-1993.* (Concordia College, Moorhead, MN), p. 62-64.

12. Especially "Moral Sensitivity," p. 129-144.

13. Aristotle, *Nicomachean Ethics,* translated by Martin Oswald (Macmillan, NY, 1962) on "voluntary and involuntary actions" (1109b30-1110b3); "choice" and "deliberation" (1111b4-1113a14); and "self-control" (1117b24-1118b7).

14. *Ibid.*, 1139b18-1138b13; 1140a24-1140b30; 1142a31-1145a11.

15. Kekes, p. 78-81; *Nicomachean Ethics*, 1139a31-1139b5.

16. Cooper, p. 1-2. "The English word 'deliberation' refers to a process of working out what to do, given certain interests, aims and principles of action, together with relevant facts about the situation to be affected." p. 5.

17. *Nicomachean Ethics*, 1143a7-8.

18. Kekes, p. 146-149.

19. Kekes, p. 152; *Nicomachean Ethics*, 1139a25-32.

20. *Nicomachean Ethics*, 1112a31-34; 1112b3.

21. Cooper, p. 1-10; J.O. Urmson, *Aristotle's Ethics*. (Basil and Blackwell, Ltd, Oxford, 1988), p. 53-57.

ASSESSING THE ETHIC OF CARE AS
AN AUTHENTIC MORAL THEORY

Lisa J. Uchno
College of Health Science
University of Detroit Mercy

When we seek to incorporate moral reasoning into the substance of the professional disciplines, we may find that some of our students are using an "ethic of care" described initially by Carol Gilligan (1977, 1982) rather than, or in addition to, an "ethic of justice." As Lawrence Blum (1993) notes, the dominant Western conception of morality is one based on rights and justice, impartiality, impersonality, formal rationality, and universal principles. Blum states that this view characterizes Lawrence Kohlberg's theory of moral development (1958, 1969, 1976, 1981) and is the bedrock of two dominant Western conceptions of morality: Kantian deontology and utilitarianism. In the last decade, Gilligan has criticized Kohlberg for gender bias in his work and she and others have presented a morality based on care and relationship. Her most recent research (Gilligan, Ward, & Taylor, 1988) suggests that both sexes are able to reason through the care ethic. But, since it does not enjoy full cultural credibility, it is not accorded widespread validity. In this essay, I will summarize justice-based morality, compare and contrast the moral development theories of Kohlberg and Gilligan, and delineate basic features of feminine and feminist-based ethics as they relate to the ethic of care. I will then explore the final questions of what would be necessary to create a full-fledged theory of care, how it can be determined when to employ a justice-based perspective, and when to employ a care-based perspective; and whether a "unified" moral theory is possible. This information may help us better inform our students about the complexities of moral deliberation and affirm their own moral voice.

Traditional, Justice-Based Ethics

Rosemarie Tong summarizes traditional Western ethics as follows:

In the Western world, traditional ethics consists of those ethical systems that aim to discover, articulate, and interpret the ultimate moral principles that should govern persons' actions.

These principles are supposedly universal and impartial, governing everyone irrespective of race, class, gender, and so forth; and the persons they govern are supposedly autonomous (endowed with enough knowledge and power to be able to decide for themselves what is right and wrong). Utilitarian and deontological ethical theories have dominated the moral landscape for at least two centuries. Neither emphasizes feminine values, and neither is particularly concerned about women's subordination or liberation (1993, p. 11).

Elaborating on the "masculine" in traditional ethics, Linda Nicholson (1993) states that much of Western moral theory, independent of Kohlberg, has evidenced many characteristics which could be labelled "masculine" along the lines suggested by Gilligan (p. 91). Nicholson paraphrases Blum's position in this regard:

> Thus, for both Kant and Hegel, the following qualities define that which is moral: rationality, self-control, strength of will, consistency, acting from universal principles, and adherence to duty and obligation. Moreover, these philosophers define the morally good "man" as specifically lacking the following qualities: sympathy, compassion, kindness, caring for others, and human concern--in short, those qualities associated with the emotional component of human nature which has also been linked with femininity (p. 91).

The Moral Development Views of Kohlberg and Gilligan

Carol Gilligan has been instrumental in focusing attention on a contrasting voice in moral decision making to the foregoing traditional conception of morality. In order to understand her position, it is first necessary to summarize that of Lawrence Kohlberg, since Gilligan's objection to his conclusion about female moral reasoning served as the springboard for her ethic of care.

Joan Tronto (1993) identifies Kohlberg's cognitive-development theory as the most widely accepted theory of moral development theory today. In his research he mainly presented hypothetical moral scenarios to his subjects and rated their solutions. His model was derived from a longitudinal study of 84 boys, now being followed for approximately 25 years. The "Heinz" scenario is a well-known example of Kohlberg's methodology. In it, Heinz's wife is very ill and requires an expensive medication which the druggist has overpriced and which the couple is unable to afford. The question is posed to the subjects: Should Heinz steal the drug? Based on his research, Kohlberg (1958, 1969, 1976, 1981) determined six progressively more advanced stages of moral reasoning. A summary of the six stages follows.

Stages One and Two form the preconventional level, mainly used by children, in which rules and social expectations are perceived as being external to self. In Stage One: Punishment and Obedience, one defers to and obeys authority in order to avoid punishment. In Stage Two: Instrumental Exchange, one attempts to satisfy individual needs and allows others to do the same through cooperation and simple exchange. Stages Three and Four form the conventional level, used primarily by late adolescents and adults. They involve internalization of societal rules and expectations. In Stage Three: Interpersonal Conformity, one places mutual agreements and shared feelings over individual interests; seeking approval is very important. In Stage Four: Social System and Conscience Maintenance, one senses the importance of preserving the social good through obeying the law and carrying out one's duty. In it, relationships are subordinated to rules. Stages Five and Six form the postconventional level, in which principles of morality become vital. In Stage Five: Prior Rights and Social Contract, one adheres to basic rights and standards of morality endorsed by society at large. In Stage Six: Universal Ethical Principles, one operates from self-chosen, universal, abstract justice-based principles in ethical reasoning. Kohlberg, it should be noted, has acknowledged that he has not found sufficient empirical confirmation for Stage Six except as a theoretical construct (Colby, Kohlberg, Gibbs, & Lieberman, 1983).

Of Kohlberg's theory, Gilligan states:

Although Kohlberg claims universality for his stage sequence, those groups not included in his original sample rarely reach his higher stages. Prominent among those who thus appear to be deficient in moral development when measured by Kohlberg's scale are women, whose judgments seem to exemplify the third stage of the six-stage sequence. At this stage morality is conceived in interpersonal terms and goodness is equated with helping and pleasing others (1982, p. 18).

Catherine Greeno and Eleanor Maccoby term Gilligan's identification of this flaw in Kohlberg's research her "primary departure from the work that precedes her. She argues that although the androcentric coding system used for Kohlberg's dilemmas shows women remaining at level three more often than do men, women are not in fact fixed at this relatively immature level but progress along a path different from that followed by men" (1993, p. 194).

Gilligan, who had formerly been mentored by Kohlberg, then conducted her own research. She "[began] with a study of women and [derived] developmental constructs from their lives," arriving at an "outline of a moral conception different from that described by Freud, Piaget, or Kohlberg" (Gilligan, 1982, p. 19). Gilligan drew upon the neo-Freudian theory of psychologist Nancy Chodorow in her explanation for the strength of the ethic of care in many women. In Chodorow's theory of sex differences in personality formation, the basic developmental task of young boys is to detach themselves from their mothers and identify with their fathers (1974, 1978). This leads to traits of autonomy and independence, which, according to Gilligan, are consonant with an ethical focus in many males upon concepts such as justice, rights, fairness, and rules. On the other hand, young girls continue to identify with their mothers, leading to traits of nurturance and caretaking, which, according to Gilligan, are consonant with an ethical focus in many females upon needs, responsibility, care and relationships. Thus, in Gilligan's conception of female moral formation, the "moral problem arises from conflicting responsibilities rather than from competing rights" (Gilligan, 1982, p. 19).

As Gilligan sees it, the moral agent must take into account the context of the moral dilemma and the specific relationships involved, grapple with the inherent ambiguities, and attempt to harm no one and care for all through the decision taken (1982). This is not easy, as will be discussed later. To illustrate an example of care-based analysis, Gilligan reinterprets the responses given to Kohlbergian researchers by Jake and Amy, two eleven-year-old children, to the Heinz dilemma mentioned earlier. Gilligan shows that Amy is quite adept at moral reasoning in a care-based ethic, although Kohlberg scored her response lower than Jake's because Jake used justice-based reasoning. Jake decided that Heinz should steal the drug because he saw the problem as "sort of a math problem with humans" (p. 26), i.e., one of competing rights: the right of Heinz's wife to life over against the druggist's right to his property. Since human life has greater value than a drug, Jake believed that Heinz should steal the drug. Amy saw the problem as one involving the relationships of Heinz, his wife, and the druggist. She reasoned that if Heinz stole the drug "he might save his wife then, but if he did, he might have to go to jail, and then his wife might get sicker again, and he couldn't get more of the drug, and it might not be good. So, they should really just talk it out and find some other way to make the money" (p. 28). Amy ultimately saw the dilemma as "a failure of the druggist to respond to the wife," to exhibit an attitude of caring toward her (p. 29). Thus, in Amy's analysis, the "moral problem changes from one of unfair domination, the imposition of property over life, to one of unnecessary exclusion, the failure of the druggist to respond to the wife" (p. 32).

In Gilligan's model, there are three progressive levels of moral reasoning. They are essentially a movement from an overly self-centered position to an overly other-centered position to finally a self-in-relation-to-others position (Tong, 1993, p. 85). As Gilligan (1977) describes her model, there are three levels and two transition periods in the development of the ethic of care. In Level One: Orientation to Individual Survival, one is solely concerned with self. Survival of the self is of paramount importance and morality is a matter of imposed sanctions on the self. The First Transition: From Selfishness to Responsibility, occurs when one becomes aware of and begins to care for others. In Level Two: Goodness as Self-Sacrifice, one adopts the stereotypical view of woman as caretaker and nurturer. Concern for others' feelings and the non-infliction of hurt weigh heavily. Caring for others and seeking the approval of others is good, even to the point of self-sacrifice. The Second Transition: From Goodness to Truth, entails the awareness that one must care for self as well as for others. "The situations, the intentions, and the consequences of an action are of primary import here, not the evaluation of others" (Brabeck, 1993, p. 36). Gilligan says that a woman "strives to encompass the needs of both self and others, to be responsible to others and thus be 'good' but also to be responsible to herself and thus to be 'honest' and 'real'" (Gilligan, 1977, p. 500). In Level Three: The Morality of Non-Violence, one uses the principle of non-violence (non-infliction of hurt) and the obligation to care to resolve conflicts between the needs of the self and others. "Care then becomes a universal obligation, the self-chosen ethic of a postconventional judgment" that achieves a moral equality between the self and other (Gilligan, 1977, p. 504). To come to this moral equality requires, Blum (1993) writes, "achieving knowledge of the particular other person toward whom one acts" and is "an often complex and difficult moral task, and one which draws on specifically moral capacities" (p. 51). He goes on to state that what is required is a

> stance...informed by care, love, empathy, compassion, and emotional sensitivity. It involves, for example, the ability to see the self as different in important ways from oneself, as a being existing in her own right, rather than viewing her through a simple projection of what one would feel if one were in her situation. Kohlberg's view follows a good deal of current moral philosophy in ignoring this dimension of moral understanding, thus implying that knowledge of individual others is a straightforwardly empirical matter requiring no particular moral stance toward the person (p. 51).

In Gilligan's research reported in *In a Different Voice* (1982), she found that many women, and some men, characteristically use the ethic of care in resolving moral dilemmas, while many men, and some women, use the justice-based ethic to do so. However, in her most recent work, *Mapping the Moral Domain* (Gilligan, Ward & Taylor, 1988), she refines her theory of moral development. Analyzing several studies of children and adolescents, she reports that by age eleven, a young person is "fluent" in the language of both rights and responsibilities, but will use the approach favored by his or her peers.

The differences, then, between the Kohlberg and Gilligan moral models are these, as summarized by Brabeck (1993). For Kohlberg, the primary moral imperative is justice; for Gilligan, it is care. The components of morality in Kohlberg's model are the sanctity of the individual, the rights of self and others, fairness, reciprocity, respect, and rules/legalities. Gilligan's components of morality are relationships, responsibility for self and others, care, harmony, compassion, and the dichotomy between selfishness and self-sacrifice. An important digression is to note, as Blum (1993) does, that for Gilligan "each person is embedded within a web of ongoing relationships, and morality importantly, if not exclusively, consists in attention to, understanding of, and emotional responsiveness toward the individuals with whom one stands in these relationships" (p. 50). Blum goes on to acknowledge, "While Kohlberg does not...deny that there is an irreducible particularity in our affective relationships with others, he sees this particularity only as a matter of personal attitude and affection, not relevant to morality itself" (p. 51). The nature of moral dilemmas in Kohlberg's model consists of conflicting rights; in Gilligan, it consists of threats to harmony and relationships. The determinant of moral obligation for Kohlberg is principles; for Gilligan, it is relationships. Kohlberg's model utilizes formal, deductive reasoning. Gilligan's model primarily relies on inductive reasoning. The self is viewed as separate and individuated in Kohlberg's model, while the self is viewed as connected and attached in Gilligan's model. There is no moral role ascribed to affect by Kohlberg, but Gilligan states that affect absolutely motivates care and compassion. She also, according to Blum (1993), sees morality as "necessarily intertwining emotion, cognition, and action, not readily separable. Knowing what to do involves knowing others and being connected in ways involving both emotion and cognition. Caring action expresses emotion and understanding" (p. 52). Lastly, the philosophical orientation found in Kohlberg is rationalistic, while in Gilligan it is phenomenological (or contextual relativism).

Criticisms have been made of Gilligan's moral system that it lacks a universal principle and that it is morally relativistic. Regarding the first contention, it should be clear from Gilligan's model that her universal imperative is to care and to build relationships. Jean

Grimshaw describes this principle as being "expressed in the form of 'Consider....' Consider whether your action will harm others; consider what the consequences for other people will be if you do this; consider whether the needs of others should outweigh considerations of your own" (1986, p. 207). Blum also comments that "care for particular persons cannot be exhaustively codified into [several] universal principles" and that Gilligan's approach "acknowledges that other moral capacities [besides identification of rights and justice] involving perception and sensitivity to particulars and care and concern for individual persons are equally central to moral agency" (1993, p. 62).

On the point of moral relativism, it is true that Gilligan rejects the notion that there is one necessarily stock action appropriate to all similar situations (other than some demonstratable manifestation of care). But she is not relativistic, according to Blum. He explains:

She at least implicitly rejects, in favor of a wider notion of "appropriate response," a conception of "right action" which carries this universalistic implication. At the same time, Gilligan's view avoids the individual subjectivism and relativism which is often seen as the only alternative to a view such as Kohlberg's; for Gilligan sees the notions of care and responsibility as providing nonsubjective standards by which appropriateness of response can be appraised in the particular case. It is a standard which allows one to say that a certain thing was the appropriate action for a particular individual to take, but not necessarily that it was the "right" action for anyone in that situation (1993, p. 52).

Following a Kantian-type exceptionless moral imperative can lead to more harm than good, which Gilligan's "ethics of ambiguity" (Broughton, 1993, p. 114) may avoid. For instance, Kant would require refusing to lie to the Nazi soldiers at the door about whether the household was sheltering Jews. It surely seems contradictory that one be compelled always to follow a moral dictum which can cause immoral consequences. A judgment based on the given circumstance should be allowed in a moral system precisely to prevent immoral acts.

Basic Features of Feminine and Feminist-Based Ethics as They Relate to the Ethic of Care

Having presented Gilligan's ethic of care, a critical examination of the feminine and feminist ethics it relates to is appropriate in order better to appraise her work. Gilligan's focus upon care and responsibility in acting ethically immediately exemplifies aspects of feminine ethics. Susan Sherwin states that a feminine approach to ethics "consists of observations of how the traditional approaches to ethics fail to fit the moral experiences and intuitions of women" (1992, p. 42). Betty Sichel adds that feminine ethics "at present refers to the search for women's unique voice and most often, the advocacy of an ethic of care that includes nurturance, care, compassion, and networks of communications" (1991, p. 90). On the other hand, a feminist approach to ethics, according to Sherwin, "applies a specifically political perspective and offers suggestions for how ethics must be revised if it is to get at the patterns of dominance and oppression as they affect women" (p. 42-43). Sichel elaborates that feminist approaches "whether liberal or radical or other orientation, argue against patriarchal domination, for equal rights, a just and fair distribution of scarce resources, etc." (p. 90). Tong explains that although differences exist between these two approaches, adherents of both "tend to believe that the self is an interdependent being rather than an atomistic entity. [They] will also tend to believe that knowledge is 'emotional' as well as 'rational' and that thoughtful persons reflect on concrete particularities as well as abstract universals" (1993, p. 80).

With Gilligan's emphasis on the moral responsibility to exhibit care and concern, her moral system is feminine in nature. Dangers in exhibiting unqualified care for others might be raised against Gilligan's ethic by some feminists, since caring behavior can unfortunately symbolize to a sexist society the "rightful" subsidiary status of women. Bill Puka describes this as "a sexist service orientation, prominent in the patriarchal socialization, social conventions, and roles of many cultures" (1990, p. 59). Tong states:

Caring actions, maternal feelings, and intimate relationships are not ethically unproblematic. On the contrary, such actions, feelings and relationships may actually impede women's moral development insofar as they encourage women to become or remain subordinate to men or, for that matter, to children" (1993, p. 165).

The related problem she discusses is a cultural fostering of the view that "because women care and have cared, they should always care no matter the cost to themselves" (p. 100). Gilligan certainly fosters the elevation of women to full dignity in society. It is true, however, that she is not specific about the possibility of self-sacrificial behavior or unhealthy caring, e.g. choosing to remain in a relationship with an abusive spouse. It would seem, though, that a person at Level Three of Gilligan's ethic of care would be able to exhibit the maturity to discern when to limit unhealthy caring and destructive relationships to the extent appropriate.

So, simply because the ethic of care is so thoroughly cemented to caring behavior does not mean that Gilligan in any way endorses the subjection of women or distorted forms of caring. Through "a changed understanding of human development and a more generative view of human life," authentic caring within a non-sexist society is possible (Gilligan, 1982, p. 174). Tong reminds us: "The world would be a much worse place tomorrow than it is today were women suddenly to stop meeting the physical and psychological needs of those who depend on them" (1993, p. 103). She also comments:

> Care is worth "rescuing" from the patriarchal structures that would misuse or abuse it....Thus, genuine or fully authentic caring cannot occur under patriarchal conditions, that is, conditions characterized by male domination and female subordination. Only under conditions of sexual equality and freedom can women care for men without men in any way diminishing, disempowering, and/or disregarding them....As long as men demand and expect caring from women, both sexes will shrink morally: neither men nor women will be able to authentically care (p. 103-104).

Many of the strengths that Allison Jaggar (1991) specifies of feminist ethics are found in Gilligan's work. Jaggar identifies several ways that traditional ethics has failed women. First, traditional ethics has shown little concern for women's interests. This problem centers on what "male" ethics focuses on as moral problems. Tong gives examples, including

> women's "double day," that is, about whether it is fair that working wives do more in the way of housework than their working husbands. Likewise, traditional ethicists have not written much about the sexual abuse of women and girls outside the confines of their homes, let alone within them. Articles on marital rape, date rape, and incest either remain unwritten or are written from a defensive point of view (1993, p. 162).

Another lack of concern in traditional ethics is the denial of women as moral agents. Clearly, Gilligan supports and commends women (and men) who use the ethic of care and cites it as a long overdue source of knowledge about human moral reasoning. A third problem in Western ethics is the tendency to extol supposedly male traits such as "independence, autonomy, intellect, will, wariness, hierarchy, domination, culture, transcendence, product, asceticism, war and death" and to depreciate supposedly female traits such as "interdependence, community, connection, sharing, emotion, body, trust, absence of hierarchy, nature, immanence, process, joy, peace and life" (Jaggar, 1991, p. 364). Gilligan emphasizes many of the latter characteristics in her work. A final charge that Jaggar makes against traditional ethics is that it undervalues or devalues women's moral experiences. Jaggar urges the development of a system of ethics based on the "conviction that the subordination of women is morally wrong and that the moral experience of women is as worthy of respect as that of men" (Jaggar, p. 361). Valuing women's moral experience is precisely where Gilligan begins.

Some Final Questions

Thus far, this analysis of the ethic of care has examined Gilligan's moral conception, juxtaposing it to traditional ethics, particularly

Kohlberg's schema of moral development. Then, features of feminine and feminist ethics as they bear on Gilligan's model were presented and used to critique it. Three remaining questions to be explored are these: Is the ethic of care a full-blown ethical theory? When may it be more appropriate to use the ethic of care, and when may it be more appropriate to use the ethic of justice? Finally, what is the relationship between justice and care? Is a "unified" moral system possible, incorporating justice, care and perhaps other qualities?

What is Necessary to Create a Theory of Care-Based Ethics?

Tronto states that the following would need to be addressed by Gilligan in order to craft a complete theory of care: its metaethical nature, the limits of care, and politics and care (1993, p. 248-51). Taking each in turn, she states about the metaethical question:

> As a fully developed moral theory, the ethic of care will take the form of a contextual moral theory [as contrasted with traditional Western ethics' universalizable, abstract, impartial, generalizable moral theory]....
> Quite obviously, if such caretaking is the quintessential moral task, the context within which conflicting demands occurs will be an important factor in determining the morally correct act. To resort to abstract, universal principles is to go outside of the web of relationships. Thus, despite Kohlberg's dismissal of care as secondary to and dependent on justice reasoning, from a different metaethical perspective, care may set the boundaries of when justice concerns are appropriate (p. 249).

Regarding the limits of care and continuing with the metaethical issue, Tronto states:

> Universalistic moral theories presume that they apply to all cases; contextual moral theories must specify when and how they apply....
> This question arises because we do not care for everyone equally. We care more for those who are emotionally, physically, and even culturally closer to us. Thus, an ethic of

care could become a defense of caring only for one's own family, friends, group, nation. From this perspective, caring could become a justification for any set of conventional relationships. Any advocate of an ethic of care will need to address the questions: "What are the appropriate boundaries of our caring?" and more important, "How far should the boundaries of caring be expanded?"

Furthermore...if the preservation of a web of relationships is the starting premise of an ethic of care, then there is little basis for critical reflection on whether those relationships are good, healthy, or worthy of preservation (p. 249-50).

This final suggestion by Tronto as to what is needed in Gilligan's model to constitute it as a complete theory of care deals with questions crucial to any social and political theory. These include the following:

Where does caring come from? Is it learned in the family? If so, does an ethic of care mandate something about the need for, or the nature of, families? Who determines who can be a member of the caring society? What should be the role of the market in a caring society? Who should bear the responsibility for education? How much equality is acceptable before individuals become indifferent to those who are too different in status? How well do current institutions and theories support the ethic of care?

Finally, we need to think about how an ethic of care might be situated in the context of existing political and social theory. An ethic of care constitutes a view of self, relationships, and social order that may be incompatible with the emphasis on individual rights that is so predominant in Western liberal, democratic societies....As onerous as rights may seem when viewed from the standpoint of our desires for connected, extended selves, they do serve at least somewhat to protect oppressed individuals. While current yearnings for greater community seem to manifest a view of the self that would allow for more caring, there is nothing inherent in community that keeps it from being oppressive toward women and others. Unless feminists assume responsibility for situating the ethic of care in the context of the rights/community discussions, the end results may be that caring can be used to justify positions that feminists would find unacceptable (p. 251).

Tronto concludes that this "difficult task" of addressing these matters that surround the ethic of care will need to "[explore] the promises, as well as the problems, involved in thinking about the ethic of care as an alternative moral theory, rather than simply as a complement to traditional moral theories based on justice reasoning" (p. 252).

When May it be Appropriate to Employ the Justice-Based Framework? When May it be Appropriate to Employ the Care-Based Framework?

Some moral problems are open to both justice and care considerations. At other times, one may be more relevant than the other. Tong believes, like Gilligan, that most people can use both in a given moral dilemma: "Most individuals will find themselves interpreting a moral drama first from one of these perspectives and then from the other, but some individuals will be unable to alternate their viewpoint between the justice and care perspectives" (1993, p. 93).

As an example of the relevance of both perspectives, Owen Flanagan and Kathryn Jackson comment in regard to the "Heinz and the druggist" scenario: "Heinz, after all, should steal the drug because it is *his* wife; and his wife should get the drug because *any* human life is more important than any avaricious pharmacist's desire to make some extra money (1993, p. 74). Both justice and care perspectives are relevant to this dilemma. As another example, consider whether one should tell one's spouse the truth about an extramarital affair in the past, which would doubtless be devastating news. Or should one remain silent (presuming there is no possibility that a sexually-transmitted disease was transmitted)? There is a conflict between the justice-based spouse's right to know and the care-based protection of the spouse's feelings and preservation of the relationship. But, they also caution that in some cases, "construing a particular problem from both perspectives will block moral clarity about what should be done" (p. 59). They ask for some decision procedure to resolve such conflicts.

When there is uncertainty about which moral viewpoint, justice or care, to adopt in a particular context, Marilyn Friedman offers this "decision procedure":

Unlike the concepts of justice and care, which admit of a mutual integration, it is less clear that these two distinct forms of moral commitment can jointly comprise the focus of one's moral attention, in any single case. Nor can we respond to all other persons equally well in either way. The only integration possible here may be to seek the more intimate, responsive, committed relationships with people who are known closely, or known in contexts in which differential needs are important and can be known with some reliability, and to settle for rule-based equal respect toward that vast number of others whom one cannot know in any particularity (1993, p. 270-71).

So it seems that uncertainty is unavoidable, at least at times, in deciding whether to use one ethical approach or the other. But dilemma, after all, is inherent in moral conflicts. Whether justice and care can be joined, and whether such a gestalt composed of these and other values would be sufficient for all moral analysis, is taken up as the final topic.

Can Justice and Care be Joined? Is a Unified Moral Theory Possible?

First, there is still a widely-held misconception about Gilligan's position that should be clarified. Gilligan does not see care as superseding justice. She sees the moral validity to both moral approaches. But, according to Tong, "Like her past efforts to interrelate justice and care, Gilligan's most recent efforts have tended to fall on deaf ears. The majority of Gilligan's readers continue to hear her words as a claim that care is somehow both separate from and better than justice. Moreover, some of Gilligan's most careful readers believe that she is committed to the view that women, on account of their alleged capacity for caring, are more moral than men" (1993, p. 93-94).

On the importance of care, Tong states: "In the end, care may not be the prerogative of any one gender, as some of Gilligan's critics insist, but of any group of people who understand that without specific others, the self is a tragically impoverished, even if gloriously autonomous, creature" (1993, p. 107). Of the significance of justice, Claudia Card says that justice, properly interpreted, directs attention to the need to overcome sexism, racism, ethnocentrism, homophobia, and xenophobia (1990). A caring society, she says, is impossible until there is a just society. In rebuttal, Neil Noddings points out that justice cannot serve to correct the previously noted social sins if it "[bogs] down in endless abstract wrangling over procedural rules and definitions instead of listening and responding" (1990, p. 122). Of the joint importance of care and justice, Brabeck states:

> Morality must be concerned with what one ought to do and that "ought" must be rationally defensible. This demands attention to regulative principles as well as attention to the specific context....When Gilligan's and Kohlberg's theories are taken together, the moral person is seen as one whose moral choices reflect reasoned and deliberate judgments that ensure justice be accorded each person while maintaining a passionate concern for the well-being and care of each individual. Justice and care are then joined; the demands of universal principles and specific moral choices are bridged; and the need for autonomy and for interconnection are united in an enlarged and more adequate conception of morality (1993, p. 47-48).

So, it is hard to disagree that both justice and care are necessary in a valid morality. Can they ever be knitted up? In *In a Different Voice* (1982), Gilligan seems to speak of justice and care as forming a gestalt. She concludes that the inclusion of women's experience "enlarges the moral domain" by the "inclusion of responsibility and care in relationships....Just as the language of responsibilities provides a weblike imagery of relationships to replace a hierarchical ordering that dissolves with the coming of equality, so the language of rights underlines the importance of including in the network of care not only the other but also the self" (p. 173). She states that "in the representation of maturity, both perspectives converge in the realization that just as inequality adversely affects both parties in an unequal relationship, so too violence is destructive for everyone involved" (p. 174). Her gestalt is interpreted by Tong in this way: "Although these two perspectives cannot completely and finally converge, neither are they diametrically opposed polarities" (1993, p. 93). Blum expresses his view on this matter:

> Gilligan does not suggest that care and responsibility are to be seen either as replacing impartiality as a basis of morality or as encompassing all of morality, as if all moral concerns could be translated into ones of care and responsibility. Rather, Gilligan holds that there is an appropriate place for impartiality, universal principles, and the like within morality, and that a final mature morality involves a complex interaction and dialogue between the concerns of impartiality and those of personal relationship and care (1993, p. 50).

As an example of the "dialogue" between justice and care, consider how justice is sometimes tempered with mercy in everyday life, integrating justice-based and care-based concerns. Tong cites several examples:

> We are reluctant to punish adolescent criminals as severely as adult criminals. We sometimes give people another chance because it would be too cruel to ruin their lives on account of a single mistake. We occasionally give people more than their fair share because we want to "cheer them up" or motivate them to do even better in the future. We even forgive our enemies (1993, p. 93).

However, no matter how they are integrated, Blum does not find that justice (he terms it "impartiality") and care are sufficient for a complete moral system.

> I would myself suggest that, even taken together, care and impartiality do not encompass all there is to morality. Other moral phenomena--a random selection might include community, honesty, courage, prudence--while perhaps not constituting full and comprehensive moral orientations, are nevertheless not reducible to (though also not necessarily

incompatible with) care and impartiality. A satisfactory picture of moral maturity or moral excellence or virtue will have to go beyond the, admittedly large, territory encompassed by care and impartiality (1993, p. 58).

He alludes to virtue ethics here, but is quick to clarify that

It should not be thought that all of the concerns of a moral outlook or sensibility grounded in care and relationship can be encompassed within what currently goes by the name of "virtue theory." And the converse of this is true also...attention to some of the concerns of virtue theory, for example, an exploration of some of the different psychological capacities contributing to a lived morality of care in relationships, would enrich the care approach (p. 58).

The shortcomings he finds in virtue ethics may be related to the fact that virtue theory elaborates habits of being that make for a person of good moral character (e.g., honesty, courage, prudence, friendship), but one still needs guideposts and processes by which to direct one's way through a moral issue.

Lastly, on the broadest question of whether it is ever possible to create a unified morality through the integration of justice and care (or any other values), Flanagan and Jackson believe not. They introduce this subject as follows:

Much recent work in moral philosophy has questioned this view of morality as a clearly carved domain for which a unified theory can be produced....This means that we will have to learn to tolerate and perhaps applaud a rich diversity of good moral personalities. The fact that this will be hard for those still in the grip of the doctrine of the "unity of the moral" in no way belies the possibility that this is the right road to go (1993, p. 84).

Adding detail to this view, Thomas Nagel speaks of an existent plurality of values. He does not cite care specifically, but does note that conflicts can arise between five fundamental types of values: specific obligations to others (which could include care); general rights; the general welfare (or utility); intrinsic ends or values (e.g., the value inherent in art or science, independent of other contributions such works might make); and commitment to one's own projects or undertakings. He does not believe that there is a "unitary source of value" to which all these values can be traced back. Rather, he "[believes] that value has fundamentally different kinds of sources....[which] renders implausible any reductive unification of ethics" (1979, p. 132-33). Nagel states that these conflicts are resolved by "judgment, essentially the faculty Aristotle described as practical wisdom" employed to see the problem from different perspectives and decide which perspective or value is most relevant (p. 135). Joan Callahan describes Nagel's philosophy as a contextually-based process, recognizing a "pool of values" (1993). There is, she says, "no algorithm that supplies the answer as to which value(s) to use. In a given context, certain of these values will take priority."

Of a unified theory, Nagel, too, believes that such a quest is futile. He states: "To look for a single unified theory of how to decide the right thing to do is like looking for a single theory of how to decide what to believe" (p. 135). There "will never be such a theory, in my view, since the role of judgment in resolving conflicts and applying disparate claims and considerations to real life is indispensable" (p. 137). He further explains that judgment will indicate "the points at which different kinds of ethical considerations need to be introduced to supply the basis for a responsible and intelligent decision" (p. 139). Thus, ambiguity again muddies the moral waters, but responsible, informed judgment based on the context of the problem and the most appropriate moral values can suffice.

Conclusion

This essay has offered an examination of a new ethical perspective: the ethic of care, and has contrasted it with the traditional Western justice-based ethic. The ethic of justice is based on the autonomy of the individual. Procedurally, it uses the principles of justice and rights to resolve moral dilemmas. The ethic of care is based on caring for self and others, who are seen in a web of relationships. Procedurally, it evaluates the particulars of the context and the needs of persons involved in resolving moral dilemmas, so that hurt and injustice are minimized. The ethic of care is situated both within feminine and feminist ethics, and is, along with justice, a virtue worthy of inclusion in a virtue-based ethical approach. However, some writers maintain that the ethic of care, in order to serve as a theory, requires further development of related social, cultural and political ramifications. Ultimately, it appears that those who would hope for a single ethic incorporating justice, care and other significant virtues will need to learn to live with the impossibility of such a task. They could take a lesson from those persons whose stories Gilligan presented in her research who are able to coexist with ambiguity and can evaluate each moral situation and person affected by that moral dilemma in their uniqueness and needs. Both justice and care are valid ethical perspectives. Each makes a contribution to the totality of moral reasoning. It is important to recognize the validity of each of these ethical perspectives (and others, such as virtue ethics) with our students and develop their experience in using them in order to know which, singly or in combination, "best fit" the persons affected by the moral problems confronting them.

References

Blum, L. "Gilligan and Kohlberg: Implications for Moral Theory." M. J. Larrabee, ed. *An Ethic of Care: Feminist and Interdisciplinary Perspectives.* New York: Routledge, Chapman and Hall, 1993. 49-68.

Brabeck, M. "Moral Judgment: Theory and Research on Differences between Males and Females." M. J. Larrabee, ed. *An Ethic of Care: Feminist and Interdisciplinary Perspectives.* New York: Routledge, Chapman and Hall, 1993. 33-48.

Broughton, J. M. "Women's Rationality and Men's Virtues: A Critique of Gender Dualism in Gilligan's Theory of Moral Development." M. J. Larrabee, ed. *An Ethic of Care: Feminist and Interdisciplinary Perspectives.* New York: Routledge, Chapman and Hall, 1993. 112-139.

Callahan, J. Presentation made at National Endowment for the Humanities-sponsored "Ethics Across The Curriculum" Summer Institute, Marquette University, Milwaukee, WI, July 17, 1993.

Card, C. "Caring and Evil." *Hypatia* 5, No. 1 (Spring, 1990): 101-108.

Chodorow, N. "Family Structure and Feminine Personality." M. Z. Rosaldo and L. Lamphere, eds. *Woman, Culture and Society.* Palo Alto, CA: Stanford University Press, 1974. 43-66.

_____. *The Reproduction of Mothering.* Berkeley: University of California Press, 1978.

Colby, A., L. Kohlberg, J. Gibbs, & M. Lieberman. "A Longitudinal Study of Moral Judgment." *Monographs of the Society for Research in Child Development.* 48 (1983): 1-96.

Flanagan, O. & K. Jackson. "Justice, Care and Gender: The Kohlberg-Gilligan Debate Revisited." M. J. Larrabee, ed. *An Ethic of Care: Feminist and Interdisciplinary Perspectives.* New York:

Routledge, Chapman and Hall, 1993. 69-84.

Friedman, M. "Beyond Caring: The De-Moralization of Gender." M. J. Larrabee, ed. *An Ethic of Care: Feminist and Interdisciplinary Perspectives*. New York: Routledge, Chapman and Hall, 1993. 258-273.

Gilligan, C. "Concepts of the Self and of Morality." *Harvard Educational Review* 47. (1977): 481-517.

_____. *In a Different Voice: Psychological Theory and Women's Development*. Cambridge: Harvard University Press, 1982.

Gilligan, C., J. V. Ward and J. M. Taylor, eds. *Mapping the Moral Domain*. Cambridge: Harvard University Press, 1988.

Greeno, C. G. and E. E. Maccoby. "How Different is the 'Different Voice'?" M. J. Larrabee, ed. *An Ethic of Care: Feminist and Interdisciplinary Perspectives*. New York: Routledge, Chapman and Hall, 1993. 193-198.

Grimshaw, J. *Philosophy and Feminist Thinking*. Minneapolis: University of Minnesota Press, 1986.

Jaggar, A. "Feminist Ethics: Projects, Problems, Prospects." C. Card, ed. *Feminist Ethics*. Lawrence, KA: University of Kansas Press, 1991. 78-104.

Kohlberg, L. "The Development of Modes of Thinking and Choices in Years 10 to 16." Ph.D. Diss., University of Chicago, 1958.

_____. "Stage and Sequence: The Cognitive-Developmental Approach." D. Goslin, ed. *Handbook of Socialization Theory and Research*. Chicago: Rand McNally, 1969.

_____. "Moral Stages and Moralization." T. Likona, ed. *Moral Development and Behavior*. New York: Holt, Rinehart and Winston, 1976. 31-53.

_____. *Essays on Moral Development.* Vol. 1: *The Philosophy of Moral Development.* San Francisco: Harper and Row, 1981.

Nagel, T. *Mortal Questions.* Cambridge: Harvard University Press, 1979.

Nicholson, L. J. "Women, Morality and History." M. J. Larrabee, ed. *An Ethic of Care: Feminist and Interdisciplinary Perspectives.* New York: Routledge, Chapman and Hall, 1993. 87-101.

Noddings, N. "A Response." *Hypatia* 5, No. 1 (Spring 1990): 120-126.

Puka, B. "The Liberation of Caring." *Hypatia* 5, No. 1 (Spring 1990): 58-82.

Sherwin, S. *No Longer Patient: Feminist Ethics and Health Care.* Philadelphia: Temple University Press, 1992.

Sichel, B. A. "Different Strains and Strands: Feminist Contributions to Ethical Theory." *American Philosophical Newsletter on Feminism and Philosophy* 90, No. 2 (Winter 1991): 90.

Tong, R. *Feminine and Feminist Ethics.* Belmont, CA: Wadsworth, 1993.

Tronto, J. "Beyond Gender Differences to a Theory of Care." M. J. Larrabee, ed. *An Ethic of Care: Feminist and Interdisciplinary Perspectives.* New York: Routledge, Chapman and Hall, 1993. 240-257.

ANIMAL RIGHTS AND ANIMAL WELFARE EDUCATION

Lyle E. Westrom
Department of Animal Science
University of Minnesota - Crookston

I. Introduction

Diogenes, the Greek philosopher, when asked about the proper time to eat, replied, "If a rich man, when you will; if a poor man, when you can." Today, well-fed nations are scrambling to eat better, and hungry nations to eat at all. One-third of all the people on earth go to bed hungry each night (Ensminger, 1991).

World food distribution is an enduring problem. It is a multi-faceted ethical dilemma. It has cultural, economic, philosophical, biological, political, and legal dimensions. The ethical dilemmas can surface on many fronts. Should food be used as a weapon? Are chemicals used in food production contaminating underground water supplies? Is genetic plant diversity being lost? Should civilized societies be prepared to pay more for animal products, so that food animals can be given greater dignity, improved welfare, or perhaps "rights?"

Life is an interdisciplinary encounter. Citizens of developed nations have grown accustomed to walking into a supermarket and returning home with every item they went to buy. Little thought is given to the origin of a vegetable, be it Oregon or Mexico. Less thought is probably given to whether a chicken is raised in confinement or on open range. Less thought still is likely given to the vast majority of people in the world who do not have access to a supermarket, could not afford the food if they had access to a supermarket, and would likely find the shelves bare even if they had the money to buy them.

Life is truly an interdisciplinary encounter, and every graduate of an institution of higher education is expected to be a leader and citizen of the world. It follows that ethical dilemmas regarding the production, supply, and distribution of food should hold a place in college curricula.

This essay will focus on how institutions of higher education can incorporate ethical issues concerning animal welfare and animal rights into a curriculum. Animal welfare/animal rights was chosen because: (1) its scope is appropriate for this essay, and (2) its recent media attention has elevated the awareness of people about the issue.

II. Significance of Animal Welfare and Animal Rights

Animals are viewed from many perspectives, depending on who is thinking about them. Animals can be a source of income, a form of recreation, a natural wonder, a mode of transportation, a subject for research, a dietary staple, an artist's focal point, or a companion. Animals are hated by some and mystified by others. One factor can be agreed upon by most people; animals have a distinct presence and importance. It is with that common thread that we examine animal significance.

Animal agriculture is a primary source of income to farmers and a primary source of food and non-food products to consumers. Approximately 52% of United States farm income is derived from animals. Animals provide two-thirds of the protein eaten by consumers in the United States and over one-third of the protein eaten by people throughout the world. Since inadequate protein is the greatest cause of malnutrition in the world, animals provide a remedy that cannot be disavowed.

Throughout much of the world, the significance of animals takes the form of transportation and work. A look at the history of societies indicates that the greatest contribution animals make toward society is by allowing people more time to be creative. It is imperative that developed nations not forget the plight of developing nations in that key developmental factor.

The significance of animals as companions, entertainment, or as a natural wonder, is difficult to quantify. Seeing a grizzly bear is certainly part of the reason thousands of people visit Glacier National Park each year. Pets provide friendship and a necessary stimulus for children and elderly throughout the world.

III. Incorporating Animal Welfare and Animal Rights into a Course Curriculum

An important prerequisite for discussion of ethical issues on animal welfare and animal rights is an element of relative neutrality. One must recognize that every professor has personal biases and the culture of every college lacks some of the heterogeneity that it desires. Multiple forms of distance education provide an excellent avenue for reaching the cultural facets that are lacking in one's own environment.

The Marquette experience made me realize that many liberal arts colleges throughout the United States have no one in their culture that can adequately represent the animal production segment of society. Likewise, many colleges of agriculture cannot do justice to a philosopher's viewpoint regarding animal rights. Technology must be utilized in higher education if we are to provide the knowledge necessary for students to make decisions in rapidly changing fields of knowledge.

Agricultural ethics and, specifically, ethics related to animals can be incorporated into existing ethics courses on liberal arts campuses, since food issues touch the lives of everyone. Colleges of agriculture may need to go further by including the ethical dimension in every course. A capstone ethics course may be necessary to undergird students with enough knowledge to fulfill their obligation to provide a continued source of safe food in a questioning society.

The remainder of this essay will highlight the key areas that need attention on a collegiate level. Areas such as history can be expanded if time permits. Authors such as Friend (1990) expand this area to include other theologies and philosophies. This is acceptable and desireable if it leaves enough time for students to develop their moral reasoning skills on current issues. Animal rights and animal welfare issues along with other food/agricultural ethical issues frequently command the media spotlight. Students deserve the curriculum time to develop their thoughts on these basic life sustaining issues.

IV. An Overview of Historical Perspectives

The animal welfare and animal rights issues can arguably be traced to the domestication of animals thousands of years ago. Some domestication was initiated by animals for their own survival. Most attempts by humans to domesticate animals failed, but a few succeeded. Domestication of animals such as dogs was for the express purpose of survival. Later domesticated animals served as a food source and were used for work. This allowed people more time to develop their life-style to a higher standard which we see in more well-developed civilizations. Today, some domesticated animals are used simply for pleasure or companionship.

Some present day animal rights proponents favor the elimination of all domesticated animals. Even a cursory look at the history of domestication points out the obvious difficulty in undoing thousands of years of domestication. In addition, the elimination of domesticated animals would greatly alter the life-styles of entire highly developed civilizations. The acceptance of such a dramatic position is, at best, controversial and, at worst, confrontational. Hence, the unfolding of questions and issues can easily be seen.

Social concern for animal welfare developed approximately 200 years ago. Animal welfare originally focused on cruelty issues that led to the development of anti-cruelty laws. These laws focused on willful, malicious cruelty or neglect. Most agricultural animals, animals used in research or in rodeos, and animals being hunted or trapped did not fall under anti-cruelty statutes (Rollin, 1990). Animal welfare has taken on a broader context in more recent years to promote and foster overall health and well-being of animals. This often requires an understanding of animal behavior, psychological stress factors, and physiological stress concepts (Friend, 1990).

When examining the historical aspects of animal rights and animal welfare, one should attempt to evaluate the development of trends. European nations tend to progress through stages approximately 20-50 years prior to the United States. For example, slaughter laws went into effect during the 1930s in Europe but did not have impact in the United States until the 1960s. Present day Swedish laws that give cattle the right to graze and forbid certain forms of confinement were put into effect during the 1980s. Other examples include the United Kingdom's law requiring anesthesia for dehorning and castration if performed after 8 weeks of age and welfare regulations supported by

Swiss family farms that restrain larger, more intensive systems (Rollin, 1990).

One should not overlook the farm families and pet owners throughout the world when examining history. It is commonly accepted that most domesticated animals are loved and cared for in a far better manner than many children, elderly, or mentally handicapped human beings throughout the world. Domestication of animals would likely never have come to fruition were it not for the additional love and care that animals desire and enjoy. This author's visits to hundreds of farms with animals and homes with pets have revealed positive aspects of animal life that are being slighted by media in favor of the negative images caused by a few. Ethical issues involving animals have been intertwined with most societies throughout history, but the historical importance and significance should be kept in perspective with other societal issues.

V. The Philosophical Debate

The philosophical debate surrounding animals has three or four fronts that need examination:
1. Do animals have rights?
2. Is animal welfare reform needed?
3. Can the world food supply be enhanced by the sharing of grain between animals and humans?
4. Should animals be considered natural resources?

Do animals have rights? The discussion should begin with Tom Regan, the most unyielding animal rights philosopher. Regan states that morality in a crude form consists of a set of rules that individuals voluntarily accept. He believes that the protection of rights of children and animals should be included in this voluntary agreement since they cannot protect themselves (Regan, 1983). But on what premise does Regan give animal rights the same status as human rights?

Regan believes that "inherent value" belongs equally to all those who are experiencing subjects of life. Just as inherent value is extended to humans with less abilities, it should be extended to animals. He supports the "rights" view that denies any form of discrimination against the experiencing subjects of life (Regan, 1983).

Regan's "rights" view toward animals is by his own admission in partnership with the human rights movement. Goals of the staunch animal rights movement include total elimination of the use of animals in science, agriculture and commercial or sport hunting (Regan, 1983). Ultimately, it would mean the return of all domesticated animals to their natural state.

An extreme, but slightly more moderate philosopher is the Australian, Peter Singer. Singer defines "speciesism" as bias in favor of one's own species and against members of other species. This is really an extension of the racism and sexism concepts in humans. Singer quickly adds that extending equality from one group to another does not imply that we treat the groups exactly the same, but that they receive equal consideration (Singer, 1990).

Singer uses utilitarian philosophy espoused by Jeremy Bentham as a basis for his philosophy. Bentham identifies "suffering" as the vital characteristic that gives a being the right to equal consideration. Singer refers to sentience (the capacity to suffer and/or experience enjoyment) as the only defensible boundary of concern for the interests of others. "Pain" is one premise that Singer uses to classify animals and humans equally. Singer believes animals feel pain since they undergo similar physiological changes to that of humans when placed in a painful situation. In 1951, the British committee on cruelty to wild animals stated that "we believe that the physiological, and more particularly the anatomical, evidence fully justifies and reinforces the common sense belief that animals feel pain" (Singer, 1983).

Singer develops the philosophy that suffering is not always equal between humans and animals. Higher order thinking skills possessed by humans may cause them to suffer more since they have the ability to know and fear what lies ahead. The same higher order thinking skills may cause less suffering than animals when the condition causing the suffering is temporary in nature.

Singer espouses the viewpoint that we should give the same respect to the lives of animals that we give to the lives of those humans at a similar mental level. It is with the preceding statement that Singer prefers to answer the question, "When is it wrong to kill an animal?" Does that response leave any more room for compromise with Singer than Regan regarding animals used in agriculture, science, and for hunting? A small amount perhaps, but any compromise would need to be founded on the principles of utilitarianism.

Ashmore (1987) presents the concept of moral agents and moral patients. Moral agents are those capable of performing moral acts while moral patients are the objects or recipients of moral action. One can quickly see that most human beings are capable of being both moral agents and moral patients. When one considers a two month old baby or a severely mentally handicapped individual it becomes more likely that they can only be a moral patient. But do we extend basic human rights to infants or the mentally handicapped? In most civilized societies the answer is yes. That leaves the door open for animal rights supporters to follow with a seemingly logical question, "Shouldn't animals be given the same status?"

Is animal welfare reform needed? Animal welfarists are not accepted by the polar extreme of the animal rights/animal welfare spectrum, but they may hold the key to any animal reform that is forthcoming in the near future. What is animal welfare? The historical background would lead one to believe that animal welfare is interchangeable with terms such as "humane" or "kind" or "lacking in cruelty."

Curtis suggests that an animal's hierarchy of needs can be compared to Maslow's hierarchy of human needs. While the lower needs of animals are shared with humans, Curtis suggests that the higher needs of humans are not shared with animals. Lower needs consist of food, a tolerable environment, safety, and freedom from fear. Higher needs of animals include behavioral needs. Higher needs for humans include a sense of belonging, self-esteem, intellectual needs, respect and ultimately self-actualization. Curtis entertains the idea that an animal's behavioral needs should be met and that deprivation can occur (Curtis, 1991).

The concept of *telos* is certainly related to this discussion. Animal *telos* is a distinctive set of needs and interests (physical and behavioral), genetically encoded and environmentally expressed. This set of needs and interests determines what sort of life the animal is suited to live. The key question becomes how much telos and what form is satisfactory to society's view of acceptability regarding the animal behavioral needs.

It is a "common social ethic" that the physiological needs of animals must be met along with the provision of a safe environment (with a minimum of fear). In general, animal agriculturalists do a commendable job in meeting the physiological and safety needs of animals. Numerous groups are avidly working toward correcting the minority of violators. For example, several cooperating organizations are developing a *Reference Guide for the Care of Dairy Animals* (Malloy, 1994) as well as a *Farm Evaluation Protocol, 1994* (Boeckman, Carlson, and Greufe, 1994). Projects such as these are commendable and will likely further decrease the abuses on the bottom two levels of Curtis' Hierarchy. They also stop short of addressing the larger concern about an animal's expression of their *telos* or "behavior."

Curtis (1991) addresses the issue of the interaction that exists between an animal's environment and its behavior. While some stress prevents animal boredom, too much is detrimental. So what is too much? That depends on the predictability of an animal's environment and its richness. It is suggested that an environment that is accepted as satisfying behavioral needs is one in which animals behave as they do in a standard environment.

Indices of animal well-being will likely draw further attention in evaluation of future animal welfare. One should be cautious about assuming that animal preferences are synonymous with animal well-being; they are not! Research has shown that animals frequently choose diets that are of lower nutritious quality. More likely, animal well-being will be thought of as a range of acceptable conditions for a given species based upon an accepted norm.

Can the world food supply be enhanced by the sharing of grain between animals and humans? Proponents of vegetarianism or veganism say no! Lack of protein is considered to be the most limiting factor in the elimination of malnutrition throughout the world. Gruzalski (1983) in his support of vegetarianism states that plants yield ten times more protein per acre than it would if fed to animals for meat. He adds that the satisfaction from eating vegetables and other plants is approximately equal to the satisfaction from eating meat. In addition, animal suffering would be greatly reduced by the elimination of confinement, transportation, and slaughter of animals. Any excess grain not needed for human consumption could be shared with wildlife to increase their happiness.

Ensminger (1991) takes issue with Gruzalski on several fronts. 95% of the solar energy conversion take place in plants that are non-edible to human beings. Over 75% of the land that these non-edible plants grow on is incapable of growing cereal grains. Ruminant animals are capable of utilizing these plants efficiently with only small amounts of grain. This provides a way of harvesting non-edible plants and converting them to a form that is edible by humans. It also provides elasticity to the grain market in that more grain can be fed to animals in times of surplus and less during times of shortage. In addition to converting non-edible plants to human food, ruminants are also capable of converting non-protein nitrogen to a form that is usable by humans. Ensminger's key point is often overlooked by opponents. Proteins from animal sources have a much higher value and are more usable (digestible) by humans than proteins from plant sources. The greater value results from the amino acids needed for human growth that are not available from vegetable sources. The added digestibility and biological value of meat versus grain becomes obvious when one compares the protein available from a ton of dent corn when used for humans (94.34#) versus the alternative of using it to finish a steer and eating the meat (93.44# of protein used by humans).

Should animals be considered a natural resource of humans? Animal rights proponents like Tom Regan (1993) say that viewing animals as a human resource is a fundamental wrong in our system; Singer (1990) would call it speciesism at its worst. Others who are considered strong advocates of animals, such as Department of Natural Resource (DNR) employees, spend their lifetime managing the natural wonders of the world which include both game and non-game wildlife. It would be difficult to say that DNR employees have less concern for animals than animal rights supporters. The reality is that they see the solution to animal lifestyle enhancement from totally different philosophies.

A similar difference exists between religions throughout the world. Eastern religions often view animals as equal to humans since they believe that, upon death, humans are reincarnated as animals. Many western religions believe that humans were given dominion over animals and hence serve as resources for humans.

The issue in the United States that best highlights the issue of "animals as natural resources" is the sport hunting issue. Hunting enthusiasts maintain that hunting is now necessary as a means of wildlife management in order to prevent unnecessary overpopulation and subsequent starvation. They maintain that the economic and political climate indicates a valid support for hunting in the United States. Vitali (1990) states that hunting is ethical. The premise of his position lies in the claim that only humans have rights, since animals do not have reflective ability nor do they have the ability to be moral agents. Vitali's view of animals easily allows for management as human resources. He believes this has great ecological benefits.

Regan (1993) takes an opposing position by stating that hunting and trapping are acceptable only in the case of protection. Killing an animal for any other reason violates the rights of the animal. Regan states that treating animals as "renewable resources" is a violation of those rights.

VI. Middle Ground

Where do we go from here? Providing for the physiological and safety needs of animals is a standard that most people with differing philosophical positions can accept. Providing for the behavioral or higher level needs deserves careful analysis and appropriate action based on realistic consideration of the wide array of philosophical thought.

The physiological needs of animals brings focus to nutrition, environment, and health. Most domesticated animals are cared for nutritionally at a higher level than most human beings. The National Research Council (NRC) has scientifically documented data on the nutritional needs of various species and the content/digestibility of feeds eaten by them. Farmers and nutrition consultants utilize available information and balance rations that are carried out well in most situations. Animal agriculture has a successful history largely due to the careful attention given to nutrition. Appropriate attention and research will continue in this area.

Environmental needs of animals are centered around appropriate thermal, light, air, microbic, and social environments (Curtis 1991). Implementation of known research has been more uneven in this area. This may in part be due to the high cost and questionable economic return on some factors. Examples of past research with animal welfare in mind include plastic coating of mesh for pigs and chickens, hutches and super hutches for calves, rubber mats for horses and cows, and polyurethane curtains for cattle in northern climates. Additional research could greatly strengthen this area. While minimum space requirements have been established, they may have overlooked the interaction that space may have with microbic or social environments. Perhaps cattle on pasture have a need for symbiotic relationships with birds that keep insect pests low.

Health of animals has improved due in part to available vaccines and the implementation of preventive medicine. Further attention to prevention is still needed. Serious attention should also be given to diseases that can be reduced or eliminated by changing the way in which animals interact with their environment. Levels of stress and its relationship to animal well-being should be carefully examined. Some stress is known to improve animal health and performance while too much stress impairs health and performance. Types and quantities of stressors may interact differently with animals that are highly domesticated (such as dairy cows) versus beef cows on a remote pasture in Wyoming.

Safety needs of animals must be considered in many areas. Climate across the United States varies greatly. Appropriate shade, shelter, or ventilation are often dependent on an interaction with the normal climactic extremes of an area. In general, acceptable consideration for climate is given to animals. Unseasonable weather extremes occasionally takes animal life, but that can hardly be considered the fault of a farmer when similar loss of human life such as the 1993 floods across the upper Mississippi were not considered to be neglect by the Army Corps of Engineers. Other safety issues such as predation give rise to the question, "Whose animal welfare and/or right do we consider most highly, the agricultural animal or the predator?" If protection can be given an agricultural animal without harm to the predator, the protection should be given. It becomes more questionable when trapping, hunting, or poisoning are the means of protection. While an analysis of the economic level of damage with a government reimbursement for lost livestock is the most appropriate solution if society deems that predators should not be killed, one can quickly see that the difficulty of administering such a program makes it almost impossible to implement.

Safety from environmental threats such as stray voltage, slippery surfaces, and restraining devices are necessary and quite well adhered to by animal agriculturalists. Since any motivation for intentional violation in this area is unlikely, research should focus on further enhancement of environmental safety. History suggests it is likely that the research results will be adopted.

Violations of physiological and safety needs of animals are subject to public scrutiny and enforcement through humane societies and animal welfare regulations. Willful neglect and cruelty are cause for removal of animals.

Behavioral needs of animals is the area that needs the most attention in the years to come. Deprivation of behavioral needs or denying an animal the opportunity to express its telos is not easily punishable by law, but is a form of maltreatment. This subject will be approached from the following premises, many of which are not acceptable to the extreme polar ends of thinking regarding the animal welfare/rights issue. The premises do operate, however, from the greatest likelihood of social convention over the next generation in the United States. The premises include:

1. Animals will not be afforded human rights.
2. Animals will be held in high regard.
3. People will continue to desire to eat meat and utilize animal products given past traditions and culture.
4. Additional laws and greater enforcement for neglect and cruelty will prevail.
5. Level of income/capita in the United States is such that the majority of people will not desire to spend 10-20% more for meat and other animal products that may have been raised in non-confinement situations.

6. Niche markets will develop for wealthier, suburban consumers who view animals with a certain mystique that affords them human-like attributes (but not total human rights). These people will not become vegetarians, but will pay more for meat and animal products that they deem appropriately raised.

7. European laws aimed at enhancing animal behavioral needs will influence the U.S. to draft similar laws, but not to the same extent. The U.S. has a more heterogeneous population with a more diverse cultural base.

With the above premises established, some examples of "middle ground" with reference to the behavioral needs will be examined. The examples are representative of the type of issues that must be addressed in the near future. An exhaustive list of examples will only result if animal scientists, animal behaviorists, and philosophical researchers seriously address "middle ground" research over the next decade. The dairy industry is in the midst of a dramatic change. The industry will be forced to become more competitive on the world market. Several factors will allow the dairy industry to become more competitive economically and yet enhance an animal's behavioral needs:

1. Greater utilization of pasture through intensive grazing gives the cows more freedom and allows dairy farmers to become more competitive.

2. Lower cost cold free stall housing also gives the cows more freedom while saving large amounts of overhead dollars. Cows thrive well in a cold environment given their thick hide and hair.

3. Dehorning, castration, dew claw removal, eartagging, and supernumerary teat removal should be all completed prior to five weeks of age. European laws serve as excellent models here. Early attention to these practices are far less stressful and are considered recommended management procedures today. Violators should be fined.

4. Calf raisers report that large dairy operations frequently fail to feed calves colostrum. Current recommended practices indicate that calves need colostrum within 1-2 hours after birth if they are to obtain maximum passive immunity. Perhaps the United States needs to go beyond European laws in this area.

Swine confinement operations have become so intensive that disease outbreaks that were once very uncommon are now common. Space and ventilation recommendations are often based on tolerable levels for a short period of time (e.g. while a hog is being finished for market). This may maximize return, but does not maximize the health of hogs. It is also placing the swine industry in a position just behind the poultry industry as a target for animal rights activists. The following would enhance the animals' behavioral needs and distance the enterprise from criticism of animal activists:

1. Improve the ventilation to the level desired/recommended for workers in the operation.
2. Increase the space requirements to decrease aggressive behavior. Space requirements should include access to the outdoors during the seasons that it would be desired by the animal.
3. Require all castration, ear notching, and tail docking to be completed within 10 days of birth.
4. Swine operations should undergo a federal and/or state inspection programs similar to the dairy industry.

The equine industry has many facets. The show ring sometimes demands type patterns that are not in the best interests of the horses. Many quarter horse owner acknowledge that for several years horses were bred for a more refined bone because it was what the judges desired in the show ring. The quarter horse, however, is a heavy body stock type horse that couldn't withstand its daily rigors without a more substantive bone. The following are thoughts that would enhance the behavioral needs of horses:

1. Set show ring standards that maximize the characteristics necessary for the proper use of a horse breed.
2. Bar any owner of a race horse where misuse of drugs was proven from ever entering another horse in any horse race.
3. Require all trainers to be certified and licensed.

VII. Summary

Providing education on controversial issues is very difficult. Animal rights and animal welfare is a polarized issue that requires educational methodology designed to neutralize that polarization. Distance education technology provides an avenue to access speakers representing the broad spectrum of thought on the animal rights and animal welfare issue.

"Middle ground" is often the forgotten aspect of the animal welfare and animal rights continuum. It is imperative that it be included because as one mediator between school boards and teacher unions said, "The best settlement is a compromise that leaves both sides feeling as though they gave a little more than they originally desired." An examination of the historical aspects of the animal rights and animal welfare issues affords students the opportunity to understand why the issue is polarized. Understanding polar concepts and debating them is not enough if the "real solution set" or "middle ground" as it is called in this essay is never discussed due to a lack of knowledge or an unwillingness to take that ideological position.

The animal rights and animal welfare topic is larger than its current position in higher education curriculum. It has its roots in the lives and issues of people at the most basic levels and the most complex. Citizens of the world depend on fair representation in the educational institutions that challenge the thought processes of their future decision makers.

234   *Westrom*

References

Ashmore, R. B. (1987). *Building a Moral System.* Englewood Cliffs: Prentice-Hall.

Boeckman, S., Carlson, K., and Greute, S. (1994). *Dairy Animal Care: Farm Evaluation Protocol 1994.* Stratford, Iowa: Agri-Education, Inc.

Curtis, S. E. (1991). The Welfare of Agricultural Animals. In C.V. Blatz ed. *Ethics and Agriculture.* Moscow: University of Idaho Press.

Ensminger, M. E. (1991). *Animal Science.* Danville, IL: Interstate Publishers, Inc.

Friend, T. H. (1990). Teaching Animal Welfare in the Land Grant Universities. *Journal of Animal Science,* 68 (10), 3462-3467.

Gruzalski, B. (1993). "The Case Against Raising and Killing Animals for Food." In Miller, H. and Williams, W. eds. *Ethics and Animals.* Clifton, NJ: Humana Press.

Malloy, N. B. (1994). *Reference Guide for the Care of Dairy Animals.* Park Ridge, IL: American Farm Bureau Federation.

Regan, T. (1983). *The Case for Animal Rights.* Los Angeles: University of California Press.

Rollin, B. E. (1990). "Animal Welfare, Animal Rights and Agriculture." *Journal of Animal Science,* 68 (10), 3456-3461.

Singer, P. (1990). *Animal Liberation.* New York: Random House, Inc.

Vitali, T. (1990). "Sport Hunting: Moral or Immoral?" *Environmental Ethics,* 12, 69-82.

1992 AND 1993 SUMMER INSTITUTES ON ETHICAL THEORY AND ITS APPLICATIONS

Participants:

Dr. James A. Aune
Speech/Theater
St. Olaf College

Dr. Paul R. Boehlke
Science
Dr. Martin Luther College

Prof. Bette Mae Conkin
Language Arts
Iowa Central Community College

Prof. Richard W. Doctor
English
Muskegon Community College

Dr. Dorothy Engan-Barker
Education
Mankato State University

Prof. Patricia A. Finder-Stone
Nursing
NE Wisconsin Technical College

Prof. Paul D. Frederickson
Finance
University of Wisconsin-Oshkosh

Dr. Don J. Hoodecheck
Education
St. John's University

Dr. William J. Maakestad
Management
Western Illinois University

Dr. Janet H. Matthews
English/Reading
Milwaukee Area Technical College

Dr. Genevieve G. McBride (1992 only)
Mass Communication
University of Wisconsin-Milwaukee

Dr. William H. Moorcroft
Psychology
Luther College

Dr. Mary Navarre, O.P.
Education
Aquinas College

Dr. David A. Nuesse
Computer Science
University of Wisconsin-Eau Claire

Dr. Arthur Pontynen
Art
University of Wisconsin-Oshkosh

Dr. Laurence J. Quick
Business
Illinois Benedictine College

Dr. Donna J. Rankin
Nursing
Loyola University of Chicago

Dr. Bruce W. Stuart
History
Concordia College of Minnesota

Prof. Lisa J. Uchno
Health Management
University of Detroit Mercy

Dr. Lyle E. Westrom
Animal Science
University of Minnesota-Crookston

Directors:

Dr. Robert B. Ashmore   Philosophy   Marquette University
Dr. William C. Starr   Philosophy   Marquette University

ABOUT THE EDITORS

Robert B. Ashmore, Aristotle and Aquinas on the Good Life

Robert B. Ashmore is Professor of Philosophy and Director of the Center for Ethics Studies at Marquette University. He received his doctorate from the University of Notre Dame in 1966. His book, *Building a Moral System*, was published by Prentice-Hall in 1987. He co-edited and contributed to *Ethics Across the Curriculum: The Marquette Experience*, which was published in 1991 as an outcome of the first grant awarded by the National Endowment for the Humanities. In addition to his publications in ethical theory, Dr. Ashmore has written on business ethics, process reforms in politics, and human rights issues in the Middle East conflicts. In 1989 he was awarded Marquette's Faculty Award for Teaching Excellence. Elected alderman in the City of Mequon, Wisconsin in 1993, Ashmore also serves that community as chair of the city's Ethics Board.

William C. Starr, Kant, Mill, and the Supreme Principle of Morality

William Starr is Associate Director of the Center for Ethics Studies and Associate Professor of Philosophy at Marquette University. He received his Ph.D. from the University of Wisconsin-Madison. Before coming to Marquette, he held teaching appointments at Queens University of Belfast and Penn State. He both teaches and publishes in the areas of moral, legal, and political philosophy. In addition to the present volume, he has co-edited two previous books. They are (with Richard Taylor) *Moral Philosophy: Historical and Contemporary Essays* and (with Robert Ashmore) *Ethics Across the Curriculum: The Marquette Experience*.

ABOUT THE CONTRIBUTORS

James Arnt Aune, Beyond PC: The Ethics of Classroom Controversy

James Arnt Aune is Associate Professor of Communication at the University of St. Thomas in St. Paul, Minnesota. He received his B.A. from St. Olaf College and his M.A. and Ph.D. from Northwestern University. He has taught at St. Olaf College, Tulane University, and the University of Virginia. He teaches courses in argumentation, legal communication, and the history of rhetoric. Aune is the author of several articles on rhetorical theory and a book, *Rhetoric and Marxism* (Boulder, CO: Westview Press, 1994).

Paul R. Boehlke, Integrating Ethics into Introductory Biology

Paul R. Boehlke received his Ph.D. from the University of Iowa. He is a Professor of Biology at Martin Luther College in New Ulm, Minnesota, teaching general biology, anatomy and physiology. Recent articles include "Sexuality and Sexual Ethics" and "Sexually Transmitted Diseases" in an encyclopedia to be published by Salem Press in 1994. His educational efforts in health and safety have received awards from the governor of Minnesota (1989) and The American Association for the Advancement of Science (1993).

Richard Doctor, Moral Literacy: Integrating Ethics and Freshman English

Richard Doctor completed his undergraduate work at Wheaton College, Illinois, received his Master's degree in English literature from the University of Illinois at Chicago, and has done additional graduate studies at Governors State University, Illinois, Grand Valley State University, Michigan, and Western Michigan University, Michigan. He teaches composition and literature at Muskegon Community College, Michigan. Doctor is active in the Michigan Liberal Arts Network for Development, and has been a leader in the state's community college general education reform movement.

Dorothy Engan-Barker, Challenging the Receptacle Model of Education

Dorothy Engan-Barker teaches in the area of social and philosophical foundations of education at Mankato State University, Mankato, Minnesota. She received her Ph.D. from the University of Minnesota, Minneapolis. Her research has focused on the concept of "school" as a non-democratic system and its relationship to student alienation and apathy. She is currently involved in a study which examines the ethical dimensions of instructional processes in higher education.

Patricia Finder-Stone, Weaving Ethical Threads into the Nursing Curriculum Fabric

Patricia Finder-Stone, R.N., M.S., is an instructor at Northeast Wisconsin Technical College in Green Bay where she teaches students both in the Associate Degree Nursing Program and in Allied Health Occupations. Her teaching and research interests include ethical issues related to health care reform, oncology and gerontology. She serves on the boards of Wisconsin Nurses Association, League of Women Voters of Wisconsin and American Cancer Society-Wisconsin Division. Finder-Stone is a frequent lecturer on ethical issues throughout northeast Wisconsin.

William Maakestad, Business Ethics and White Collar Crime: Blueprint for an Interdisciplinary Course

William Maakestad, Professor of Management at Western Illinois University, received his B.A. from Monmouth College and J.D. from Valparaiso University. He is author of numerous articles on the legal responsibilities of business and co-author of *Corporate Crime Under Attack: The Ford Pinto Case and Beyond*. In addition to his teaching and research duties, he coordinates the College of Business Honors Program at WIU.

Mary Navarre, **Implementing Ethics Across the Curriculum**

Mary Navarre, Ed.D., Professor of Education and Humanities, has taught at Aquinas College in Grand Rapids, Michigan since 1977. Her graduate degrees are from Oakland University in Rochester, Michigan and Boston University. She participated in the National Institute on Values and Education in 1991, sponsored by the Council of Independent Colleges. Recently, Dr. Navarre was appointed to serve on the college's Committee on Ethics and Catholic Teaching and currently is serving on the ad hoc committee for the revision of the General Education Program at the college. Dr. Navarre has published articles in both humanities and education and has taught in the college-sponsored Ireland Overseas Program in 1979 and again in 1989.

Arthur Pontynen, **Beauty vs. Aesthetics: Ethics in the Fine Arts Curriculum**

Arthur Pontynen, assistant professor in the Department of Art, the University of Wisconsin, Oshkosh, earned his Ph.D. degree in Art History at the University of Iowa in 1983, and has been a Smithsonian Fellow. Co-author of *Contemporary Painting and Calligraphy from the Republic of China* (National Palace Museum, Taiwan, 1980), he has published articles in the *Art Bulletin*, *Oriental Art*, *Field Museum Bulletin*, *Measure*, *American Arts Quarterly* (forthcoming), and *The Dictionary of Art* (forthcoming).

Laurence J. Quick, **Teaching Business Ethics to Undergraduate Management Students**

Dr. Laurence J. Quick is Associate Professor in the Department of Economics and Business, and Director of the Center for Ethics in Business at Illinois Benedictine College. He holds the B.S.C. from DePaul University, and M.M. and Ph.D. from Northwestern University. He is also a CPA. His research interests are in the areas of business ethics and U.S. global industrial competitiveness.

Bruce W. Stuart, Moral Development and Freshman Studies

Bruce Stuart received his Ph.D. in American Studies from the University of Minnesota. He currently is an Assistant Professor of History at Concordia College, Moorhead, Minnesota. He teaches United States History, freshman studies (Principia), and a research course in Environmental Studies. He also collaborates with Iris Stuart in projects that focus on pedagogical aspects of ethics and accounting.

Lisa J. Uchno, Assessing the Ethic of Care as an Authentic Moral Theory

Lisa J. Uchno until recently was assistant professor and director of the Health Information Management Program at the University of Detroit Mercy, where her courses included total quality management, fundamentals of medical science, health care management, and health care law. Her courses integrated ethical considerations within the professional discipline and incorporated general education outcomes. An additional focus of interest was the adult learner and the use of non-traditional teaching/learning methodologies. She is author of a research study on this subject. Uchno is now directing a community health status improvement project in metropolitan Detroit.

Lyle E. Westrom, Animal Rights and Animal Welfare Education

Lyle E. Westrom is Assistant Professor of Animal Science at the University of Minnesota, Crookston. He received his Ph.D. from Mississippi State University and his M.A. from the University of Minnesota, St. Paul. His focus in the revised baccalaureate mission at the University of Minnesota, Crookston includes teaching and research in dairy science and agricultural ethics. Collaboration with the University of Manitoba and distance education (ITV) with area Minnesota colleges are included in his responsibilities. Westrom is on an interdisciplinary research team studying management intensive grazing in moderate sized sustainable dairy operations.